Mindful Moments: Essential Meditations for Mental Wellbeing

Negoita Manuela

Published by Negoita Manuela, 2024.

While every precaution has been taken in the preparation of this book, the publisher assumes no responsibility for errors or omissions, or for damages resulting from the use of the information contained herein.

MINDFUL MOMENTS: ESSENTIAL MEDITATIONS FOR MENTAL WELLBEING

First edition. April 2, 2024.

Copyright © 2024 Negoita Manuela.

ISBN: 979-8224762095

Written by Negoita Manuela.

Table of Contents

Chapter 1: Introduction

- WHAT IS MINDFULNESS?

Mindfulness is a concept that has gained widespread popularity in recent years, particularly in the fields of psychology, mental health, and self-improvement. However, the term can often be misunderstood or misinterpreted, leading to confusion about what it actually entails. In essence, mindfulness is the practice of being fully present and engaged in the moment, without judgment or distraction. It involves paying attention to our thoughts, feelings, bodily sensations, and the world around us with openness and acceptance.

One of the key components of mindfulness is the focusing of our attention on the present moment. This means letting go of regrets about the past and worries about the future, and instead, fully experiencing and enjoying what is happening right now. By cultivating this awareness of the present moment, we can develop a greater sense of clarity, focus, and calmness in our everyday lives. This can help us to better handle stress, anxiety, and other challenges that may arise, as we learn to respond to situations with greater awareness and intention.

Another important aspect of mindfulness is the practice of acceptance and non-judgment. This means acknowledging our thoughts and emotions without trying to change or suppress them, and instead, allowing them to come and go without attaching any value judgments to them. By learning to observe our thoughts and feelings in this way, we can develop a greater sense of self-awareness and inner peace. This can be particularly helpful in dealing with negative emotions such as anger, sadness, or fear, as we learn to accept and navigate these feelings without allowing them to overwhelm us.

Mindfulness can be practiced through a variety of techniques, such as meditation, deep breathing exercises, body scans, and mindful movement practices like yoga or Tai Chi. These techniques can help to cultivate a sense of mindfulness and presence in our everyday lives, allowing us to bring greater awareness and intention to our actions and choices. By incorporating mindfulness practices into our daily routines, we can learn to live with greater awareness, compassion, and resilience.

Research has shown that mindfulness can have a wide range of benefits for both our physical and mental health. Studies have found that regular mindfulness practice can reduce stress, anxiety, and depression, as well as improve overall well-being and quality of life. It can also enhance cognitive abilities such as attention, memory, and decision-making, and promote greater emotional regulation and resilience in the face of challenges. Additionally, mindfulness has been found to have positive effects on physical health, such as reducing blood pressure, improving immune function, and promoting better sleep. By learning to focus on the present moment with openness and acceptance, we can develop a deeper understanding of ourselves and the world around us. Through mindfulness practices such as meditation, breathing exercises, and mindful movement, we can bring greater clarity, calmness, and resilience to our daily experiences. In doing so, we can transform our relationship with stress, anxiety, and other challenges, and learn to live with greater awareness, compassion, and equanimity.

- Benefits of mindfulness

Mindfulness is a practice that has garnered significant attention in recent years for its numerous benefits on mental, emotional, and physical well-being. Defined as the state of being fully present and aware of one's thoughts, feelings, bodily sensations, and surrounding environment, mindfulness has roots in ancient Eastern philosophies such as Buddhism and has been adapted and studied in Western psychology in the form of Mindfulness-Based Stress Reduction (MBSR) and other therapeutic modalities. The benefits of mindfulness are wide-ranging and have been documented in numerous scientific studies, making it a valuable tool for individuals seeking to improve their overall quality of life.

One of the key benefits of mindfulness is its ability to reduce stress and promote relaxation. In today's fast-paced world, many individuals find themselves overwhelmed by the demands of work, relationships, and daily responsibilities. Chronic stress can have a detrimental impact on both physical and mental health, leading to a host of conditions such as anxiety, depression, high blood pressure, and even heart disease. By practicing mindfulness, individuals learn to be present in the moment and cultivate a sense of calm awareness that can help them cope with stress more effectively. Through techniques such as deep breathing, body scanning, and mindful meditation, individuals can decrease the activation of the body's stress response system and induce a state of deep relaxation. This can have a profound impact on overall well-being and help individuals build resilience in the face of life's challenges.

In addition to its stress-reducing effects, mindfulness has been shown to improve mental health by enhancing emotional regulation and reducing symptoms of anxiety and depression. By cultivating non-judgmental awareness of their thoughts and emotions, individuals can learn to respond to difficult situations with greater clarity and equanimity. This can help break the cycle of negative thinking patterns and prevent rumination on past or future events that contribute to feelings of anxiety and depression. Mindfulness has also been shown to increase self-compassion and acceptance, allowing individuals to be kinder and more forgiving to themselves in the face of setbacks or failures. By fostering a greater sense of emotional resilience and flexibility, mindfulness can help individuals navigate the ups and downs of life with greater ease and grace.

Another important benefit of mindfulness is its impact on cognitive function and attentional control. In today's digital age, many individuals find themselves constantly bombarded by distractions and information overload, leading to a fragmented and scattered mind. By practicing mindfulness, individuals can improve their ability to focus and sustain attention on the present moment. Research has shown that mindfulness training can lead to structural changes in the brain, specifically in regions associated with attention, self-regulation, and emotion processing. This can result in improvements in working memory, executive function, and decision-making skills. By training the mind to be more focused and present, individuals can enhance their cognitive abilities and perform better in academic, professional, and personal pursuits.

Furthermore, mindfulness has been shown to have positive effects on physical health and well-being. Research has demonstrated that mindfulness can reduce inflammation in the body, lower blood pressure, and improve immune function. By reducing the body's stress response system, mindfulness can protect against the harmful effects of chronic stress on the cardiovascular and immune systems. Mindfulness has also been shown to promote healthier lifestyle behaviors, such as improved sleep quality, healthier eating habits, and increased physical activity. By fostering a greater sense of awareness and self-care, individuals can make more conscious choices that support their overall health and well-being. By cultivating a practice of present-moment awareness and non-judgmental acceptance, individuals can reduce stress, enhance emotional regulation, improve attentional control, and promote overall health and well-being. Whether through formal mindfulness meditation practices, mindful movement activities such as yoga or tai chi, or simply integrating moments of mindfulness into daily activities, individuals can tap into the transformative power of mindfulness to enhance their quality of life and cultivate a greater sense of peace, balance, and resilience.

- How to practice mindfulness

Mindfulness is a practice that has gained significant attention in recent years for its potential to improve mental and physical well-being. It involves the intentional focus on the present moment, without judgment or attachment to our thoughts or emotions. Research has shown that incorporating mindfulness into our daily routines can reduce stress, anxiety, and depression, as well as improve focus, memory, and overall quality of life.

One way to practice mindfulness is through meditation. Meditation involves sitting quietly and focusing on your breath, a mantra, or a particular sensation in the body. The goal is to bring your attention back to the present moment whenever your mind starts to wander. This can be challenging at first, as our minds are naturally wandering and distracted, but with practice, you can train your brain to be more present and focused.

Another way to practice mindfulness is through body scan exercises. This involves bringing awareness to each part of your body, starting at your toes and working your way up to your head. Notice any sensations, tension, or discomfort in each area without judgment. This can help you become more in tune with your body and recognize when you are feeling stressed or anxious.

Mindfulness can also be practiced through everyday activities such as eating, walking, or even washing dishes. By bringing your full attention to the task at hand, you can experience the present moment more fully and cultivate a sense of calm and peace. For example, when eating, pay attention to the taste, texture, and smell of the food. Notice how it feels in your mouth and how your body responds to it. This can help you savor your meals and eat more mindfully.

One important aspect of mindfulness is self-compassion. It involves treating yourself with kindness and understanding, especially when you are struggling or facing difficult emotions. Mindfulness can help you become more aware of your thoughts and feelings, and how they impact your well-being. By practicing self-compassion, you can learn to respond to yourself with care and empathy, rather than criticism or judgment.

In addition to formal meditation practices, there are many ways to incorporate mindfulness into your daily life. For example, you can practice mindful breathing exercises throughout the day, taking a few moments to focus on your breath and bring yourself back to the present moment. You can also practice mindfulness while walking, by paying attention to the sensation of your feet on the ground, the sights and sounds around you, and the movement of your body.

Mindfulness can also be practiced through journaling or reflective writing. Take a few minutes each day to write about your thoughts, feelings, and experiences. This can help you gain insight into your emotions, patterns of thinking, and behaviors, and cultivate a greater sense of self-awareness. Reflecting on your experiences can also help you process difficult emotions and gain perspective on challenging situations. By focusing on the present moment without judgment, incorporating mindful practices into your daily life, and cultivating self-compassion, you can reduce stress, anxiety, and depression, improve focus and memory, and enhance your overall quality of life. So, take some time each day to practice mindfulness and experience the many benefits it has to offer.

Chapter 2: Understanding Emotions

- RECOGNIZING AND ACCEPTING emotions

Recognizing and accepting emotions is a crucial aspect of emotional intelligence and overall well-being. Emotions play a significant role in how we perceive and interact with the world around us. They provide valuable information about our needs, desires, and values, and can influence our thoughts, behaviors, and decision-making. By being able to recognize and accept our emotions, we can better understand ourselves, communicate effectively with others, and navigate the complexities of our inner world.

One of the first steps in recognizing and accepting emotions is becoming aware of our emotional experiences. This involves paying attention to our feelings and bodily sensations, and identifying the emotions that arise in different situations. This self-awareness allows us to differentiate between different emotions and understand their underlying causes. For example, we may feel anxious before giving a presentation at work, or sad after receiving disappointing news. By recognizing these emotions, we can begin to explore the reasons behind them and take appropriate action to address them.

Once we have identified our emotions, it is important to accept them without judgment or criticism. This means acknowledging the validity of our feelings, even if they are unpleasant or uncomfortable. It is natural to experience a range of emotions, both positive and negative, and it is essential to allow ourselves to feel and express them without fear of rejection or condemnation. By accepting our emotions, we can learn from them and work towards resolving any underlying issues that may be contributing to our emotional experiences.

In addition to recognizing and accepting our own emotions, it is also crucial to be able to recognize and empathize with the emotions of others. This skill, known as emotional intelligence, enables us to understand and respond appropriately to the feelings of those around us. By recognizing and validating the emotions of others, we can build stronger relationships, foster empathy and compassion, and communicate more effectively. This is especially important in professional settings, where emotional intelligence can enhance teamwork, leadership, and conflict resolution.

There are several strategies that can help us to recognize and accept our emotions more effectively. Mindfulness practices, such as meditation and deep breathing exercises, can help us to tune into our emotional experiences and cultivate a sense of inner calm and acceptance. Journaling can also be a helpful tool for processing and reflecting on our feelings, allowing us to gain insight into our emotions and explore their deeper meanings. Seeking support from a therapist or counselor can provide additional guidance and perspective on how to navigate complex emotional issues and develop healthier coping strategies. By becoming more aware of our emotions and accepting them without judgment, we can gain insight into our inner world, communicate effectively with others, and cultivate healthier relationships. Developing these skills takes time and practice, but the benefits are significant and long-lasting. By embracing our emotions and honoring our feelings, we can live more authentically and fully engage with the world around us.

- Managing overwhelming emotions

Managing overwhelming emotions is a crucial skill that everyone should strive to develop in order to lead a more balanced and fulfilling life. Emotions are a natural and integral part of the human experience, but when they become too intense or overwhelming, they can interfere with our daily functioning and overall well-being. Whether it's anger, fear, sadness, or anxiety, learning how to effectively manage and regulate our emotions can help us navigate challenging situations with greater ease and resilience.

One of the first steps in managing overwhelming emotions is to increase our awareness and understanding of them. This involves recognizing and labeling our emotions as they arise, as well as identifying the triggers that may be contributing to their intensity. By becoming more mindful of our emotional experiences, we can begin to develop a greater sense of control and agency over how we respond to them. Mindfulness practices, such as meditation and deep breathing exercises, can be particularly helpful in cultivating this awareness and promoting emotional regulation.

In addition to increasing our awareness of our emotions, it's important to develop healthy coping strategies that can help us regulate and diffuse intense emotions when they arise. These strategies may include engaging in physical activities such as exercise or yoga, seeking support from loved ones or a therapist, journaling or expressing our emotions through creative outlets, or practicing relaxation techniques such as progressive muscle relaxation or guided imagery. Finding what works best for us individually is key in developing a personalized toolkit for managing overwhelming emotions.

Another important aspect of managing overwhelming emotions is learning how to reframe and re-evaluate our thoughts and beliefs that may be contributing to their intensity. Often, our emotions are closely tied to the stories we tell ourselves about a situation or event, and by challenging and reframing these narratives, we can gain a more balanced and objective perspective. Cognitive-behavioral techniques, such as cognitive restructuring and thought challenging, can be particularly effective in helping us identify and change the negative and irrational thoughts that may be fueling our overwhelming emotions.

It's also important to remember that it's okay to seek support from others when dealing with overwhelming emotions. Talking to a trusted friend, family member, or mental health professional can provide us with a fresh perspective and valuable insights on how to better manage our emotions. Additionally, participating in support groups or seeking out online resources and self-help books can also be helpful in developing new coping skills and strategies for handling overwhelming emotions.

Ultimately, managing overwhelming emotions is a skill that requires practice, patience, and self-compassion. It's important to remember that it's okay to feel overwhelmed at times and that it's a normal part of the human experience. By increasing our awareness, developing healthy coping strategies, reframing our thoughts and beliefs, and seeking support from others, we can learn to navigate our emotions with greater ease and flexibility, leading to a more balanced and resilient way of being.

- Cultivating emotional balance through mindfulness

Emotional balance is a key component of overall well-being and mental health. It refers to the ability to manage and regulate one's emotions in a healthy and adaptive way. Emotions play a crucial role in our daily lives, influencing how we think, feel, and behave. When we are able to cultivate emotional balance, we are better equipped to cope with stress, handle challenges, and maintain positive relationships with others.

One effective way to cultivate emotional balance is through the practice of mindfulness. Mindfulness is the practice of being fully present and engaged in the moment, without judgment or attachment to our thoughts and feelings. It involves paying attention to our thoughts, emotions, and bodily sensations with a sense of curiosity and openness. By cultivating mindfulness, we can develop a greater awareness of our emotions and a greater capacity to respond to them in a skillful and compassionate way.

Research has shown that mindfulness can have a profound impact on emotional balance. Studies have found that mindfulness practice can lead to reductions in stress, anxiety, and depression, while increasing feelings of well-being, self-compassion, and emotional regulation. By bringing awareness to our emotions through mindfulness, we can learn to observe them without becoming overwhelmed or reactive. This can help us to break free from automatic, habitual patterns of reacting to our emotions and instead respond in a more intentional and skillful way.

One of the key benefits of mindfulness in cultivating emotional balance is its ability to help us develop greater emotional resilience. Emotional resilience refers to the ability to bounce back from setbacks, cope with stress, and adapt to change. When we practice mindfulness, we become more attuned to our emotional experiences and learn to navigate them with greater ease and flexibility. This can help us to develop a sense of inner strength and stability, even in the face of challenging circumstances.

Mindfulness can also help us cultivate a greater sense of emotional intelligence. Emotional intelligence is the ability to recognize, understand, and manage our own emotions, as well as the emotions of others. By practicing mindfulness, we can develop a greater awareness of our own emotional states and learn to respond to them with greater compassion and wisdom. This can enhance our relationships with others, as we become more attuned to their emotional needs and better able to communicate and connect with them in a meaningful way.

Incorporating mindfulness into our daily lives can be a powerful tool for cultivating emotional balance. There are many different ways to practice mindfulness, including meditation, yoga, and mindful breathing exercises. These practices can help us to become more present and aware of our thoughts, emotions, and bodily sensations. By integrating mindfulness into our daily routines, we can learn to cultivate a greater sense of inner calm and stability, even in the midst of life's ups and downs. By developing greater awareness of our emotions and learning to respond to them in a skillful and compassionate way, we can increase our emotional resilience, enhance our emotional intelligence, and foster deeper connections with others. Through regular mindfulness practice, we can cultivate a greater sense of inner peace and presence, leading to a more fulfilling and meaningful life.

Chapter 3: Body Scan Meditation

- EXPLORING SENSATIONS in the body

Sensations in the body are an integral part of our human experience, playing a significant role in how we perceive and interact with the world around us. From the feeling of a cool breeze on our skin to the rush of adrenaline during moments of excitement, sensations help us navigate our environment and make sense of our internal state. Exploring sensations in the body involves delving deep into the complex web of sensory information that our nervous system processes every moment of our waking lives.

One of the primary sensory systems responsible for detecting and relaying information about the body's internal and external environment is the somatosensory system. This intricate network of specialized nerve cells, known as sensory receptors, is distributed throughout the skin, muscles, joints, and internal organs. These receptors are sensitive to various stimuli, such as touch, temperature, pressure, vibration, and pain, and send signals to the brain for processing and interpretation. By understanding the function and organization of the somatosensory system, we can gain insight into how our bodies perceive and respond to different sensations.

Touch is one of the most fundamental sensations experienced by the body, providing vital information about our surroundings and facilitating social interactions. The sense of touch is mediated by a diverse array of sensory receptors located in the skin, each responding to specific types of tactile stimuli. Mechanoreceptors, for example, detect pressure, vibration, and texture, while thermoreceptors sense changes in temperature. These receptors work in concert to create a rich tapestry of tactile sensations that inform us about the qualities of objects we touch, the temperature of our environment, and the presence of potential threats or dangers.

Pain is another essential sensation that serves a protective function, alerting us to potential tissue damage or injury. The experience of pain is complex and multifaceted, involving both sensory and emotional components. Nociceptors, specialized nerve fibers that respond to noxious stimuli, are responsible for detecting potentially harmful signals and transmitting them to the brain for processing. In addition to its role in signaling tissue damage, pain can also be influenced by psychological and emotional factors, such as stress, anxiety, and past experiences. By exploring the nuances of pain perception, we can develop a more nuanced understanding of how our bodies respond to and cope with discomfort.

Beyond touch and pain, the body also experiences a wide range of proprioceptive sensations that provide information about our body's position, movement, and posture. Proprioception is the sense that allows us to coordinate our movements, maintain balance, and navigate our environment with precision. Proprioceptive signals are generated by specialized receptors located in the muscles, tendons, and joints, and are integrated with information from the visual and vestibular systems to create a cohesive sense of body awareness. By honing our proprioceptive abilities through activities such as yoga, dance, or martial arts, we can enhance our kinesthetic sense and improve our overall physical performance.

In addition to the somatosensory system, the body also receives and processes information from other sensory modalities, such as vision, hearing, taste, and smell. These sensory inputs work in concert to create a holistic picture of our environment and our internal state. For example, the integration of visual and proprioceptive cues helps us maintain balance and coordination, while the combination of taste and smell informs our perception of flavor. By exploring the interactions between different sensory modalities, we can deepen our understanding of how the brain synthesizes information from multiple sources to create a unified sensory experience. By studying the somatosensory system, we can unravel the mysteries of touch, pain, and proprioception, gaining insight into how our bodies perceive and respond to the world around us. As we delve deeper into the nuances of sensory processing, we can develop a more profound appreciation for the intricate interplay of sensory inputs that shape our perception of reality. By embracing the richness and depth of our sensory experiences, we can cultivate a greater sense of awareness, presence, and connection with ourselves and the world at large.

- Relaxing the body and mind

Relaxation is an essential component of maintaining overall health and well-being. Many people lead busy and stressful lives, which can take a toll on both the body and mind. It is important to take time to relax and unwind in order to recharge and rejuvenate. There are many different ways to relax the body and mind, and finding the right method for you is key to achieving a state of relaxation.

One way to relax the body and mind is through meditation. Meditation is a practice that has been used for centuries to promote relaxation and inner peace. By focusing on your breath and clearing your mind of distractions, you can achieve a sense of calm and serenity. Meditation can be done anywhere and at any time, making it a convenient and effective way to relax.

Another way to relax the body and mind is through mindfulness. Mindfulness is the practice of being present in the moment and paying attention to your thoughts and feelings without judgment. By practicing mindfulness, you can reduce stress and anxiety, improve your mood, and enhance your overall well-being. Mindfulness can be practiced through formal meditation exercises or simply by being fully present in everyday activities such as eating, walking, or talking to a friend.

Yoga is another effective way to relax the body and mind. Yoga combines physical postures, breathing techniques, and meditation to promote relaxation, flexibility, and strength. By practicing yoga regularly, you can reduce stress, improve your mood, and increase your sense of well-being. Yoga can be tailored to suit your individual needs and abilities, making it a versatile and accessible form of relaxation.

Engaging in physical activity is also a great way to relax the body and mind. Exercise releases endorphins, which are chemicals in the brain that act as natural painkillers and mood elevators. By engaging in regular physical activity, you can reduce stress, improve your mood, and increase your overall sense of well-being. Whether you prefer to go for a run, take a dance class, or practice yoga, finding a form of exercise that you enjoy can help you relax and unwind.

Spending time in nature is another effective way to relax the body and mind. Nature has a calming effect on the body and mind, and spending time outdoors can reduce stress, improve mood, and increase feelings of happiness and well-being. Whether you go for a hike in the woods, relax by the ocean, or simply sit in a park and soak up the sunshine, spending time in nature can help you relax and rejuvenate. There are many different ways to relax, from meditation and mindfulness to yoga, exercise, and spending time in nature. Finding the right method for you is key to achieving a state of relaxation that works for you. By taking the time to relax and unwind, you can recharge and rejuvenate your body and mind, leading to improved health and well-being.

- Improving mind-body connection

The mind-body connection is a complex and multifaceted relationship that plays a crucial role in our overall health and well-being. It refers to the intricate interplay between our thoughts, emotions, and physical sensations, and how they influence each other. When this connection is strong and healthy, we are better able to cope with stress, manage our emotions, and maintain a sense of balance and harmony in our lives. However, when this connection is weak or disrupted, it can lead to a host of physical and mental health problems, such as chronic pain, anxiety, depression, and other chronic health conditions.

Improving the mind-body connection is essential for promoting overall health and wellness. There are several strategies that can help strengthen this connection, including mindfulness practices, relaxation techniques, physical exercise, and healthy lifestyle choices. Mindfulness practices, such as meditation, yoga, and deep breathing exercises, can help us become more aware of our thoughts and feelings, and how they impact our physical sensations. By practicing mindfulness regularly, we can learn to stay present in the moment, reduce stress and anxiety, and improve our overall emotional well-being.

Physical exercise is another important component of improving the mind-body connection. Regular exercise has been shown to have numerous benefits for both our physical and mental health, including reducing stress, boosting mood, and improving sleep quality. When we engage in physical activity, our bodies release endorphins, which are chemicals that act as natural painkillers and mood boosters. By incorporating regular exercise into our daily routine, we can strengthen our mind-body connection and improve our overall well-being.

In addition to mindfulness practices and physical exercise, making healthy lifestyle choices can also help improve the mind-body connection. Eating a balanced diet, getting enough sleep, and avoiding unhealthy habits such as smoking and excessive alcohol consumption can all have a positive impact on our overall health and well-being. When we take care of our bodies, we are better able to cope with stress, regulate our emotions, and maintain a sense of balance and harmony in our lives.

It is important to remember that improving the mind-body connection is a process that takes time and practice. It requires a commitment to making positive changes in our lives, and a willingness to explore new ways of thinking and being. By incorporating mindfulness practices, physical exercise, and healthy lifestyle choices into our daily routine, we can strengthen our mind-body connection and improve our overall health and well-being. By improving this connection through mindfulness practices, physical exercise, and healthy lifestyle choices, we can enhance our ability to cope with stress, manage our emotions, and maintain a sense of balance and harmony in our lives. It is important to approach this process with an open mind and a willingness to explore new ways of thinking and being. By making a commitment to improving our mind-body connection, we can achieve a greater sense of well-being and vitality.

Chapter 4: Breath Awareness

- FOCUS ON THE BREATH as a meditation anchor

Meditation has been practiced for thousands of years as a way to cultivate mindfulness, focus, and inner peace. One common technique used in meditation is to focus on the breath as an anchor for the mind. This simple yet powerful practice involves paying attention to the sensations of breathing in and out, using the breath as a focal point to bring the mind into the present moment. By anchoring our awareness on the breath, we can quiet the chatter of the mind, reduce stress, and improve our overall well-being.

Focusing on the breath as a meditation anchor is a fundamental practice in many traditional meditation traditions, such as Vipassana, Zen, and Mindfulness meditation. It is a technique that can be easily accessible to anyone, regardless of their level of experience with meditation. The breath is always with us, providing a constant and reliable anchor for our attention. By directing our awareness to the breath, we can train the mind to stay focused and present, rather than being caught up in distractions or worries.

One of the key benefits of using the breath as a meditation anchor is its ability to help us cultivate mindfulness. Mindfulness is the practice of paying deliberate, non-judgmental attention to the present moment. When we focus on the breath, we are training our minds to be fully present and aware of what is happening in the here and now. This can help us develop a greater sense of clarity, calm, and equanimity, even in the midst of life's challenges.

Another benefit of using the breath as a meditation anchor is its ability to calm the nervous system and reduce stress. When we are stressed or anxious, our breath tends to become shallow and rapid. By consciously slowing down and deepening our breath through meditation, we can activate the body's relaxation response, leading to a sense of calm and ease. This can be particularly helpful for those struggling with anxiety, insomnia, or chronic pain.

Furthermore, focusing on the breath as a meditation anchor can help improve our concentration and focus. In our fast-paced, technology-driven world, it is easy to become distracted and overwhelmed by the constant barrage of information and stimuli. By training our minds to stay present with the breath, we can strengthen our ability to sustain attention and avoid getting caught up in distractions. This can lead to increased productivity, creativity, and overall mental clarity. By cultivating mindfulness, reducing stress, improving concentration, and fostering inner peace, we can enhance our overall quality of life and sense of happiness. Whether you are a seasoned meditator or new to the practice, incorporating the breath as a meditation anchor can serve as a valuable tool for finding greater balance and presence in your daily life.

- Deepening the breath for relaxation

One of the most effective and accessible ways to induce a state of relaxation is through deepening the breath. By consciously engaging with the breath and deepening its rhythm and depth, individuals can activate the body's relaxation response, leading to a decrease in stress levels, a sense of calmness, and improved overall well-being. In this discussion, we will explore the mechanisms behind deepening the breath for relaxation, the benefits it offers, and practical techniques that can be implemented to incorporate deep breathing into daily life.

To begin, it is essential to understand how deepening the breath can promote relaxation. The act of taking deep breaths engages the diaphragm, which is the primary muscle responsible for respiration. When we take shallow breaths, we rely mainly on the muscles in the chest and shoulders, which can contribute to increased tension and stress. By actively engaging the diaphragm and allowing it to descend fully during inhalation, we can increase the amount of oxygen entering the body and promote greater relaxation. Deep breathing also stimulates the parasympathetic nervous system, which is responsible for slowing the heart rate, reducing blood pressure, and promoting a sense of calmness and relaxation.

The benefits of deepening the breath for relaxation are numerous and far-reaching. Research has shown that deep breathing can help to reduce anxiety, improve mood, and enhance cognitive function. By increasing oxygen intake and engaging the diaphragm, deep breathing can also improve respiratory function and lung capacity. Additionally, deep breathing has been found to support the body's natural detoxification processes by aiding in the removal of waste gases and improving circulation. Regular practice of deep breathing can also help to build resilience to stress and cultivate a greater sense of mindfulness and presence in daily life.

There are several techniques that can be utilized to deepen the breath and induce a state of relaxation. One of the most straightforward methods is diaphragmatic breathing, also known as abdominal breathing. To practice diaphragmatic breathing, begin by finding a comfortable seated or lying position. Place one hand on your chest and one hand on your abdomen. As you inhale through your nose, allow your abdomen to expand fully, pushing your hand out. As you exhale through your mouth, gently contract your abdomen, allowing your hand to move back towards your body. Continue this deep breathing pattern for several minutes, focusing on the sensation of expansion and contraction in your abdomen.

Another effective technique for deepening the breath is box breathing, which involves equal counts for inhalation, hold, exhalation, and hold. Begin by inhaling deeply through your nose for a count of four, holding your breath for a count of four, exhaling through your mouth for a count of four, and holding your breath for a count of four. Repeat this cycle for several minutes, focusing on the rhythmic pattern of your breath. Box breathing can help to calm the mind, reduce anxiety, and promote a sense of centeredness and balance. By engaging with the breath and incorporating deep breathing techniques into daily life, individuals can tap into the body's natural relaxation response, reduce stress levels, and cultivate a greater sense of calmness and presence. Whether practicing diaphragmatic breathing, box breathing, or other relaxation techniques, the key lies in developing a regular and consistent practice that allows for deepening the breath and harnessing its transformative power. By taking the time to connect with our breath and honor its capacity for promoting relaxation, we can create a foundation for greater health, balance, and vitality in our lives.

- Enhancing mindfulness through breath awareness

In recent years, mindfulness has gained widespread attention for its numerous benefits on mental and physical well-being. One powerful technique for cultivating mindfulness is breath awareness. By focusing on the breath and being fully present in the moment, individuals can enhance their ability to be mindful in their daily lives. This practice allows individuals to connect with the present moment, increase self-awareness, and reduce stress and anxiety. In this paper, we will explore the concept of enhancing mindfulness through breath awareness, including its benefits, techniques, and practical applications.

Breath awareness is a fundamental mindfulness practice that involves paying attention to the breath as it moves in and out of the body. The breath serves as an anchor for the mind, allowing individuals to focus their attention and bring awareness to the present moment. By observing the breath without judgment, individuals can cultivate a sense of calm and clarity, leading to greater mindfulness in their daily lives. This practice harnesses the power of the breath, which is an integral part of our existence and serves as a constant reminder of our connection to the present moment.

One of the key benefits of enhancing mindfulness through breath awareness is its ability to reduce stress and anxiety. When individuals become more attuned to their breath, they can regulate their emotions and create a sense of calm and relaxation. By focusing on the present moment and letting go of worries about the past or future, individuals can experience a greater sense of peace and well-being. Research has shown that regular practice of breath awareness can lead to decreased levels of stress hormones, improved mood, and enhanced overall mental health.

In addition to reducing stress, breath awareness can also help individuals increase their self-awareness and emotional intelligence. By tuning into the subtle sensations of the breath, individuals can learn to recognize patterns of thoughts, emotions, and behaviors that may be contributing to stress or anxiety. This heightened awareness can help individuals make more conscious choices in their daily lives and respond to challenges with greater clarity and compassion. By cultivating this self-awareness through breath awareness, individuals can develop a deeper understanding of themselves and their inner world.

Practicing breath awareness can also improve cognitive function and focus. By training the mind to stay focused on the breath, individuals can strengthen their ability to concentrate and maintain attention on tasks. This enhanced focus can lead to greater productivity, creativity, and overall mental clarity. Research has shown that regular practice of mindfulness techniques, such as breath awareness, can improve cognitive function, memory, and decision-making skills. By incorporating breath awareness into their daily routine, individuals can enhance their cognitive abilities and achieve a greater sense of mental clarity and focus.

There are several techniques that individuals can use to enhance mindfulness through breath awareness. One simple and effective technique is to find a quiet and comfortable place to sit or lie down. Close your eyes and bring your attention to your breath, noticing the sensation of the air entering and leaving your body. You can focus on the rise and fall of your chest or the feeling of the breath moving in and out of your nostrils. As thoughts, emotions, or distractions arise, simply acknowledge them and gently return your focus to the breath. By practicing this technique regularly, individuals can strengthen their mindfulness muscle and experience the numerous benefits of breath awareness. By focusing on the breath and being fully present in the moment, individuals can reduce stress, increase self-awareness, improve cognitive function, and enhance emotional intelligence. Through regular practice of breath awareness, individuals can cultivate a greater sense of mindfulness in their daily lives and experience increased peace, clarity, and well-being. By incorporating breath awareness into their daily routine, individuals can harness the power of the breath and cultivate a deeper connection to the present moment.

Chapter 5: Loving-Kindness Meditation

- CULTIVATING COMPASSION for oneself and others

Cultivating compassion for oneself and others is a critical aspect of emotional intelligence and overall well-being. Compassion is defined as a deep awareness of and sympathy for another's suffering, along with a desire to alleviate that suffering. It involves empathizing with others, showing kindness and understanding, and offering support and care. When we extend compassion towards ourselves, we acknowledge our own struggles and imperfections with gentleness and understanding. By practicing self-compassion, we become better equipped to show compassion towards others, fostering stronger relationships and creating a more compassionate world.

To cultivate compassion for oneself, it is essential to first recognize that we are all imperfect and deserving of kindness and understanding. Self-compassion involves treating ourselves with the same level of care and empathy that we would offer to a dear friend in need. This means acknowledging our mistakes and shortcomings without harsh self-criticism or judgment. It also involves recognizing our own humanity and inherent worth, regardless of our flaws or failures. By practicing self-compassion, we can develop a greater sense of self-acceptance and resilience, enabling us to navigate life's challenges with greater ease and grace.

One effective way to cultivate self-compassion is through mindfulness practices. Mindfulness involves paying attention to the present moment with curiosity and non-judgment. By practicing mindfulness, we can become more aware of our thoughts, feelings, and sensations, helping us to recognize when we are being self-critical or unkind to ourselves. Mindfulness allows us to cultivate a greater sense of self-awareness and self-compassion, enabling us to respond to our own suffering with kindness and understanding.

Another important aspect of cultivating self-compassion is to practice self-care. Self-care involves taking care of our physical, emotional, and mental well-being by engaging in activities that nourish and replenish us. This may include getting enough rest, nourishing our bodies with healthy food, engaging in activities that bring us joy and relaxation, and seeking support from others when needed. By prioritizing self-care, we can cultivate a greater sense of self-compassion and well-being, enabling us to show up more fully in our relationships and in the world.

In addition to cultivating self-compassion, it is equally important to extend compassion towards others. Compassion for others involves empathizing with their struggles, offering support and kindness, and striving to alleviate their suffering in any way we can. By practicing compassion towards others, we can foster stronger relationships, cultivate a greater sense of empathy and connection, and contribute to a more compassionate and caring world.

One way to cultivate compassion towards others is through acts of kindness and generosity. This may involve volunteering your time or resources to help those in need, offering a listening ear to a friend or loved one who is struggling, or simply showing kindness and empathy towards strangers in your community. By engaging in acts of kindness and generosity, we can cultivate a greater sense of compassion and connection towards others, creating a ripple effect of positivity and care in our lives and in the world.

Another important aspect of cultivating compassion towards others is to practice active listening and empathy. Active listening involves truly hearing and understanding the perspectives and emotions of others without judgment or interruption. By practicing active listening, we can cultivate a greater sense of empathy and connection towards others, enabling us to respond with kindness and understanding to their needs and struggles. This can help to strengthen our relationships, build trust and rapport with others, and create a more compassionate and caring community. By practicing self-compassion, mindfulness, and self-care, we can develop a greater sense of self-acceptance and resilience, enabling us to navigate life's challenges with greater ease and grace. By extending compassion towards others through acts of kindness, generosity, active listening, and empathy, we can foster stronger relationships, cultivate a greater sense of empathy and connection, and contribute to a more compassionate and caring world. In doing so, we can create a ripple effect of positivity and care that benefits not only ourselves but also those around us.

- Fostering empathy and connection

Fostering empathy involves understanding and sharing the feelings of others, while connection refers to the emotional bond that develops between individuals. These two concepts are interconnected and play a crucial role in building strong, meaningful relationships with others.

One way to foster empathy and connection is through active listening. Active listening involves fully engaging with the speaker, paying attention to their words, tone, and body language. By actively listening, you show that you value and respect the other person's perspective, which can help build trust and deepen the connection between you. Additionally, active listening can help you understand the emotions behind the speaker's words, allowing you to respond with empathy and compassion.

Another way to foster empathy and connection is through perspective-taking. Perspective-taking involves putting yourself in the other person's shoes, trying to understand their thoughts, feelings, and experiences. This practice can help you see things from their point of view, leading to increased empathy and a stronger connection. By considering the perspective of others, you can build more meaningful relationships and cultivate a greater sense of understanding and compassion.

Empathy and connection can also be fostered through effective communication. Open and honest communication is key to building trust and fostering connection with others. By expressing your thoughts and feelings openly and listening attentively to others, you can create a safe space for emotional expression and vulnerability. This can deepen the bond between individuals and strengthen the connection between them. Additionally, effective communication can help resolve conflicts and misunderstandings, leading to healthier and more fulfilling relationships.

Practicing self-compassion is another important way to foster empathy and connection. Self-compassion involves treating yourself with kindness, understanding, and acceptance, especially in times of struggle or difficulty. By cultivating self-compassion, you can develop a deeper sense of empathy for yourself, which can in turn lead to greater empathy and connection with others. When you are kind and compassionate towards yourself, you are better able to extend that same kindness and compassion to others, fostering stronger, more meaningful relationships.

In addition to these strategies, participating in acts of kindness and service can also help foster empathy and connection. By engaging in acts of kindness, such as volunteering or helping others in need, you can cultivate a greater sense of empathy and compassion for those around you. These acts of kindness not only benefit others but also bring a sense of fulfillment and connection to the person performing them. By actively seeking out opportunities to help and support others, you can deepen your empathy and connection with the world around you. By practicing active listening, perspective-taking, effective communication, self-compassion, and acts of kindness, you can cultivate a deeper sense of empathy and connection with those around you. These practices can lead to healthier, more fulfilling relationships and a greater sense of well-being for both yourself and those you interact with. By prioritizing empathy and connection in your interactions with others, you can create a more compassionate and interconnected world.

- Spreading positivity through loving-kindness

Spreading positivity through loving-kindness is a concept that has been embraced by many cultures and religions throughout history. The practice of loving-kindness, also known as metta in the Buddhist tradition, involves cultivating feelings of goodwill, compassion, and kindness towards all beings. This practice is believed to have a transformative effect on both the individual practicing it and those around them.

At its core, loving-kindness is about recognizing the interconnectedness of all living beings and cultivating a sense of empathy and compassion towards others. By actively extending loving-kindness towards others, we create a ripple effect of positivity that can spread far and wide. This practice is not just about making ourselves feel good, but about genuinely wishing for the well-being and happiness of all beings.

Research has shown that practicing loving-kindness can have a number of positive effects on both our physical and mental health. Cultivating feelings of compassion and kindness towards others has been linked to lower levels of stress, anxiety, and depression. It can also improve our relationships with others and help us feel more connected to the world around us.

One of the key aspects of loving-kindness practice is learning to extend compassion and kindness towards ourselves. Many of us are quick to criticize ourselves and focus on our shortcomings, but by practicing loving-kindness towards ourselves, we can cultivate a sense of self-acceptance and self-love. This, in turn, can help us be more compassionate towards others.

In a world that can often feel divided and chaotic, spreading positivity through loving-kindness is more important than ever. By cultivating feelings of empathy and compassion towards others, we can help create a more harmonious and interconnected world. This practice is not about ignoring the negative aspects of life, but about choosing to respond to them with kindness and compassion.

There are many ways to incorporate loving-kindness into our daily lives. One simple practice is to silently recite phrases of loving-kindness towards ourselves and others. These phrases can be as simple as "May I be happy, may you be happy, may all beings be happy." By repeating these phrases regularly, we can train our minds to cultivate feelings of goodwill and compassion towards all beings.

Another way to spread positivity through loving-kindness is to perform random acts of kindness towards others. This can be as simple as holding the door open for someone or paying for a stranger's coffee. These small acts of kindness can have a big impact on both the recipient and the giver, spreading positivity and creating a sense of connection between people. By cultivating feelings of compassion and kindness towards all beings, we can create a more harmonious and interconnected world. Through simple practices such as reciting loving-kindness phrases and performing random acts of kindness, we can help spread positivity and create a more compassionate society. So let us all take a moment to pause, reflect, and extend loving-kindness towards ourselves and others, knowing that by doing so, we are contributing to a more positive and compassionate world.

Chapter 6: Mindful Eating

- BRINGING AWARENESS to eating habits

Eating habits play a significant role in our overall health and well-being. It is important to bring awareness to our eating habits in order to make informed choices about our diet and lifestyle. By understanding the impact of our eating habits on our physical and mental health, we can take proactive steps to improve our overall quality of life.

One key aspect of bringing awareness to eating habits is understanding the role of nutrition in our bodies. Nutrition is the process by which our bodies obtain and use food for energy, growth, and repair. A balanced diet that includes a variety of nutrients is essential for maintaining good health. By being aware of the nutrients that our bodies need, we can make better choices about the foods we consume and ensure that we are meeting our nutritional needs.

Another important aspect of bringing awareness to eating habits is recognizing the impact of our food choices on our health. Poor eating habits, such as consuming excessive amounts of unhealthy foods high in sugar, salt, and saturated fats, can lead to a variety of health issues including obesity, heart disease, and diabetes. By being mindful of the foods we eat and making healthier choices, we can reduce our risk of developing these chronic diseases and improve our overall well-being.

In addition to the physical health implications, our eating habits can also have a significant impact on our mental health. Research has shown that a poor diet can contribute to mood swings, low energy levels, and even symptoms of depression and anxiety. By paying attention to our eating habits and making healthier choices, we can support our mental health and emotional well-being. Eating a balanced diet rich in fruits, vegetables, whole grains, and lean proteins can help to stabilize mood, boost energy levels, and improve overall mental clarity.

Bringing awareness to our eating habits also involves recognizing the social and environmental factors that influence our food choices. Our food choices are often influenced by cultural traditions, family preferences, and societal norms. By being aware of these influences, we can make more conscious decisions about the foods we eat and break free from unhealthy eating patterns. Additionally, being mindful of the environmental impact of our food choices, such as choosing locally sourced and sustainably produced foods, can help to reduce our carbon footprint and support a more sustainable food system. By understanding the role of nutrition, recognizing the impact of our food choices on our health, supporting our mental health, and considering the social and environmental factors that influence our food choices, we can make informed decisions about our diet and lifestyle. By taking the time to reflect on our eating habits and make positive changes, we can improve our overall quality of life and support a healthier future for ourselves and our communities.

- Enjoying food mindfully

Enjoying food mindfully is a practice that involves paying full attention to the eating experience, from the flavors and textures of the food to the physical sensations and emotions that arise during and after a meal. This approach to eating has gained popularity in recent years as a way to promote a healthier relationship with food and cultivate a greater appreciation for the nourishment it provides. In this essay, we will explore the principles of mindful eating, discuss the benefits of adopting this practice, and provide practical tips for incorporating mindful eating into your daily routine.

Principles of Mindful Eating:

At its core, mindful eating is about being present in the moment and fully engaging with the act of eating. This means slowing down and savoring each bite, paying attention to the colors, smells, and tastes of the food, and noticing how it makes you feel physically and emotionally. Mindful eating also involves being aware of your hunger and fullness cues, so you can eat when you are truly hungry and stop when you are satisfied. By bringing a non-judgmental and curious attitude to the eating experience, you can better understand your relationship with food and make choices that support your health and well-being.

Benefits of Mindful Eating:

There are numerous benefits to practicing mindful eating, both physical and psychological. One of the key advantages is that it can help you maintain a healthy weight by preventing overeating and promoting better digestion. By tuning into your body's signals of hunger and fullness, you can avoid mindless snacking and emotional eating, leading to more balanced and satisfying meals. Mindful eating can also improve your relationship with food by reducing feelings of guilt or shame around eating and allowing you to experience pleasure and satisfaction in your meals. Additionally, research has shown that mindfulness practices like mindful eating can lower stress levels, improve mood, and enhance overall well-being.

Practical Tips for Incorporating Mindful Eating:

If you're interested in trying out mindful eating, there are several practical tips you can follow to get started. One of the first steps is to create a calm and inviting eating environment, free from distractions like phones or television. This allows you to focus on the sensory experience of eating and fully appreciate the flavors and textures of your food. When eating, take small bites and chew slowly, paying attention to the taste and mouthfeel of each bite. Try to notice any thoughts or emotions that arise as you eat, without judgment, and return your focus to the present moment. You can also practice mindful eating by being mindful of your portion sizes and making choices that align with your body's hunger and fullness cues. Over time, these small changes can help you develop a more mindful approach to eating and cultivate a greater sense of gratitude and enjoyment for the nourishment food provides. By bringing awareness and intention to the eating experience, you can savor the flavors, textures, and aromas of your food, as well as the physical and emotional sensations that arise during and after a meal. Mindful eating can help you cultivate a healthier relationship with food, support your overall well-being, and promote a greater appreciation for the nourishment that food provides. So, why not give it a try and see how mindful eating can enhance your daily meals and bring more joy and satisfaction to your eating experience.

- Building a healthy relationship with food

Building a healthy relationship with food is essential for overall well-being and long-term health. In today's fast-paced and convenience-driven society, it can be easy to fall into patterns of unhealthy eating habits. However, taking the time to develop a positive and balanced relationship with food is crucial for maintaining both physical and mental health.

One of the first steps in building a healthy relationship with food is to practice mindful eating. This involves being present and fully engaged with your meal, focusing on the tastes, textures, and sensations of the food you are consuming. By being mindful while eating, you can better listen to your body's hunger and fullness cues, which can help prevent overeating and promote a healthier relationship with food. Additionally, practicing mindfulness can also help you to savor and enjoy your food more, leading to a more satisfying dining experience.

In addition to practicing mindful eating, it is important to focus on consuming a balanced and varied diet. This means including a wide range of foods from all food groups, such as fruits, vegetables, whole grains, lean proteins, and healthy fats. Eating a variety of foods ensures that your body receives the necessary nutrients it needs to function optimally. Additionally, consuming a balanced diet can help prevent deficiencies and improve overall health.

Another key aspect of building a healthy relationship with food is to be kind to yourself and avoid labeling foods as "good" or "bad." All foods can fit into a healthy diet in moderation, and depriving yourself of certain foods can lead to feelings of guilt and shame. Instead of restricting or demonizing certain foods, focus on incorporating a wide range of foods into your diet while practicing moderation. By allowing yourself to enjoy all foods in moderation, you can develop a more positive and balanced relationship with food.

It is also important to listen to your body and honor your hunger and fullness cues. This means eating when you are hungry and stopping when you are satisfied, rather than eating based on external cues or emotions. By tuning into your body's signals, you can better regulate your food intake and prevent overeating. Additionally, practicing intuitive eating can help you develop a greater sense of self-awareness and self-trust when it comes to making food choices.

In addition to focusing on the quality and quantity of the food you consume, it is also important to consider the context in which you eat. Eating in a calm and relaxed environment can help promote healthy digestion and enjoyment of your meals. Avoiding distractions such as television, phones, or work while eating can allow you to fully focus on your food and the experience of eating. By creating a peaceful and mindful eating environment, you can enhance your overall relationship with food and promote a healthier relationship with eating.

Lastly, seeking support from a registered dietitian or therapist can be helpful in building a healthy relationship with food. These professionals can provide guidance, encouragement, and personalized recommendations to help you develop a positive relationship with food. They can also help you navigate any challenges or barriers you may face in your journey towards better eating habits. By working with a knowledgeable and supportive professional, you can gain the tools and insights needed to build a healthy and sustainable relationship with food.

Chapter 7: Walking Meditation

- PRACTICING MINDFULNESS in motion

Mindfulness in motion refers to the practice of being fully present and aware of our thoughts, feelings, and surroundings while engaged in physical activity. This practice encourages individuals to focus on the present moment and cultivate a deeper connection between the mind and body. By incorporating mindfulness into our movements, we can enhance our overall well-being and performance in various activities.

One of the key principles of mindfulness in motion is the idea of paying attention to our breath. Our breath serves as a constant anchor that helps us stay grounded and focused on the present moment. By concentrating on our breath as we move, we can regulate our emotions, reduce stress, and improve our physical performance. Simply taking a few deep breaths before engaging in any physical activity can help us center ourselves and prepare for a more mindful experience.

Another important aspect of practicing mindfulness in motion is observing our thoughts and sensations without judgment. This involves being curious and open to whatever arises during our movements, whether it be physical discomfort, distracting thoughts, or emotions. Instead of reacting impulsively to these experiences, we can simply observe them with a sense of detachment and non-judgment. By cultivating this attitude of acceptance and self-compassion, we can develop a healthier relationship with our bodies and become more in tune with our internal states.

Incorporating mindfulness into our movements can also help us improve our overall physical awareness and coordination. When we are fully present and focused on our body movements, we can better understand our body's capabilities and limitations. This increased awareness allows us to move more efficiently and gracefully, reducing the risk of injury and enhancing our performance in various activities. By tuning into the subtle cues and sensations of our body, we can ensure that we are moving in a way that is safe and aligned with our physical needs.

Furthermore, mindfulness in motion can help us cultivate a sense of flow and ease in our movements. When we are fully present and engaged in the present moment, we can enter a state of flow where our actions feel effortless and natural. This state of flow can lead to a deeper sense of enjoyment and fulfillment in our physical activities, as we are fully immersed in the experience without any distractions or self-imposed limitations. By letting go of any preconceived notions or expectations, we can allow our movements to unfold organically and authentically, leading to a more harmonious and joyful experience.

In summary, practicing mindfulness in motion offers a multitude of benefits for our physical, mental, and emotional well-being. By incorporating mindfulness into our movements, we can enhance our overall awareness, coordination, and performance in various activities. This practice encourages us to be fully present and engaged in the present moment, allowing us to cultivate a deeper connection between the mind and body. By paying attention to our breath, observing our thoughts without judgment, and moving with a sense of flow and ease, we can experience a more fulfilling and enriching physical experience. Mindfulness in motion is not just about the physical movements themselves, but about the way in which we engage with and appreciate our bodies in motion. By integrating mindfulness into our daily physical activities, we can enhance our overall well-being and lead a more balanced and mindful lifestyle.

- Connecting with the environment

Connecting with the environment is essential for our well-being and the health of the planet. As humans, we are inherently connected to the natural world, and our actions have a profound impact on the environment. Developing a strong connection with nature can lead to improved mental and physical health, as well as a greater understanding and appreciation of the natural world. In this essay, we will explore the importance of connecting with the environment, how to cultivate a strong connection to nature, and the benefits of doing so.

One of the key reasons why connecting with the environment is important is that it helps us to appreciate the beauty and diversity of the natural world. When we spend time in nature, whether it be hiking in the mountains, walking along the beach, or simply sitting in a park, we are able to witness the wonders of the earth firsthand. This can help us to feel a sense of awe and wonder at the complexity and beauty of the natural world, and can inspire us to protect and preserve it for future generations.

Furthermore, connecting with the environment can have a positive impact on our mental and physical health. Numerous studies have shown that spending time in nature can reduce stress, anxiety, and depression, and improve overall well-being. The sights, sounds, and smells of nature can have a calming effect on the mind, helping to reduce feelings of stress and overwhelm. In addition, being in nature often involves physical activity, such as hiking or gardening, which can improve fitness levels and overall health.

In addition to the benefits for individuals, connecting with the environment is also essential for the health of the planet. As humans, we are reliant on the natural world for our food, water, and air, and our actions have a significant impact on the health of the environment. By developing a connection with nature, we are more likely to adopt sustainable practices in our daily lives, such as recycling, conserving water, and reducing our carbon footprint. This can help to reduce our impact on the environment and contribute to the health and well-being of the planet as a whole.

There are several ways to cultivate a strong connection with the environment. One of the most effective ways is simply to spend time in nature on a regular basis. This could involve going for a walk in a local park, camping in the wilderness, or simply spending time in your backyard or garden. By immersing yourself in the sights, sounds, and smells of the natural world, you can begin to develop a deeper appreciation and connection to the environment.

Another way to connect with the environment is to learn more about the natural world and the issues facing it. This could involve reading books or articles about nature and conservation, attending environmental events or workshops, or volunteering with local conservation organizations. By educating yourself about the natural world and the challenges it faces, you can develop a greater understanding of the importance of protecting and preserving the environment. By developing a strong connection with nature, we can gain a greater appreciation for the beauty and diversity of the natural world, improve our mental and physical health, and contribute to the health and well-being of the planet as a whole. There are many ways to cultivate a connection with the environment, including spending time in nature, learning more about the natural world, and adopting sustainable practices in our daily lives. By taking steps to connect with the environment, we can help to create a more sustainable and healthy future for ourselves and future generations.

- Finding peace and presence through walking meditation

In today's fast-paced and chaotic world, finding moments of peace and presence can seem like a challenging task. The constant demands of work, family, and social obligations can leave us feeling overwhelmed and disconnected from ourselves. However, one powerful practice that can help us cultivate a sense of calm and mindfulness is walking meditation. This ancient practice has been used for centuries as a way to calm the mind, strengthen the body, and cultivate a deeper sense of presence in each moment.

Walking meditation involves walking slowly and intentionally while paying close attention to each step and the sensations in the body. It is a form of moving meditation that can help us connect more deeply with our surroundings and ourselves. By bringing awareness to each step and breath, we can quiet the mind and bring a sense of calm and clarity to our daily lives. Walking meditation is a simple yet profound practice that can be done anywhere, at any time, making it accessible to people of all ages and fitness levels.

One of the key benefits of walking meditation is its ability to help us cultivate a sense of presence and awareness in the present moment. In our busy lives, we often find ourselves caught up in the past or worrying about the future, which can lead to feelings of anxiety and stress. By focusing on each step and breath in the present moment, we can train our minds to be more present and attentive to what is happening right now. This can help us let go of worries and distractions, allowing us to experience a greater sense of peace and clarity.

In addition to promoting mindfulness and presence, walking meditation can also have physical benefits. The slow and deliberate pace of walking meditation can help improve balance, posture, and flexibility. It can also strengthen the muscles in the legs and promote overall cardiovascular health. By combining the physical benefits of walking with the mental benefits of meditation, walking meditation offers a holistic approach to health and well-being.

To practice walking meditation, find a quiet and peaceful place where you can walk without distractions. Begin by standing still and taking a few deep breaths to center yourself. Then, start walking slowly and mindfully, paying attention to each step as it touches the ground. Notice the sensation of your feet touching the earth, the movement of your legs and arms, and the rhythm of your breath. If your mind starts to wander, gently bring your awareness back to the present moment and continue walking with intention and focus.

As you continue to practice walking meditation, you may begin to notice a sense of calm and peace washing over you. By bringing mindfulness to each step and breath, you can quiet the chatter of your mind and cultivate a sense of inner stillness. This can help you feel more grounded and centered, even in the midst of chaos and uncertainty. Walking meditation can be a powerful tool for managing stress, anxiety, and overwhelm, allowing you to find moments of peace and presence in the midst of a busy and hectic world. By bringing mindfulness to each step and breath, we can quiet the mind, strengthen the body, and connect more deeply with ourselves and the world around us. Whether you are new to meditation or a seasoned practitioner, walking meditation offers a gentle and accessible way to find moments of stillness and clarity in the midst of a busy and hectic world. Give it a try and see how this ancient practice can help you find peace and presence in each step you take.

Chapter 8: Body Image and Self-Acceptance

- EMBRACING BODY POSITIVITY

Body positivity is a movement that has gained significant traction in recent years, aiming to challenge societal beauty standards and promote self-love and acceptance of all body types. This movement encourages individuals to embrace their bodies as they are, without feeling the need to conform to unrealistic ideals of beauty perpetuated by the media and societal expectations. While it may seem like a simple concept, embracing body positivity involves a deep internal shift in mindset and beliefs about oneself and others.

One of the key tenets of body positivity is the idea that all bodies are worthy of love and respect, regardless of size, shape, color, or ability. This includes embracing diversity and celebrating the unique beauty of each individual, rather than promoting a one-size-fits-all standard of beauty. By challenging the notion that there is only one "ideal" body type, body positivity encourages individuals to appreciate the natural diversity of human bodies and recognize that beauty comes in many different forms.

Embracing body positivity also involves debunking the myth that our worth as individuals is determined by our physical appearance. In a society that often equates beauty with value, it can be challenging to separate our self-worth from our appearance. Body positivity encourages individuals to shift their focus from external validation to internal acceptance, recognizing that our value as human beings lies in our inherent worth and unique qualities, rather than our physical appearance.

Another important aspect of body positivity is challenging harmful stereotypes and stigmas surrounding body size, shape, and appearance. This includes addressing fatphobia and promoting body inclusivity for individuals of all sizes. By challenging these harmful stereotypes, body positivity aims to create a more inclusive and accepting society where all bodies are celebrated and respected.

It is important to note that body positivity is not about promoting unhealthy behaviors or dismissing the importance of health. Rather, it is about recognizing that health looks different for everyone and that it is possible to prioritize health and well-being without obsessing over achieving a certain physical ideal. Body positivity encourages individuals to focus on self-care and self-compassion, rather than self-criticism and negative self-talk.

In order to embrace body positivity, it is important to practice self-compassion and challenge negative thoughts and beliefs about our bodies. This can be a challenging process, especially in a society that bombards us with unrealistic images of beauty and perfection. However, by cultivating a mindset of self-acceptance and self-love, we can begin to shift our perspective and embrace our bodies as they are.

One of the ways to cultivate body positivity is through positive affirmations and self-care practices. This can include repeating affirmations such as "I am worthy just as I am" or "My body is beautiful and deserving of love and respect." These affirmations can help to counteract negative self-talk and promote a more positive and accepting attitude towards our bodies.

In addition, practicing self-care activities that make us feel good in our bodies can also help to promote body positivity. This can include engaging in activities that bring us joy and connection, such as yoga, dance, or meditation. By taking care of our bodies and prioritizing our emotional well-being, we can begin to cultivate a more positive and accepting attitude towards ourselves.

It is also important to surround ourselves with positive and supportive influences that promote body positivity. This can include following body-positive influencers on social media, reading books and articles that challenge societal beauty standards, and engaging in conversations with others who share similar values. By surrounding ourselves with positive influences, we can create a supportive and encouraging environment that promotes self-acceptance and self-love. By shifting our mindset and beliefs about our bodies, we can begin to embrace and celebrate the unique beauty of each individual, promoting a more accepting and inclusive society where all bodies are respected and valued. By practicing self-acceptance and self-love, we can cultivate a more positive and empowering relationship with our bodies, leading to greater happiness and well-being in our lives.

- Overcoming negative body image

Body image is a complex and multifaceted concept that refers to how we perceive and feel about our physical appearance. Negative body image, on the other hand, occurs when individuals have a distorted perception of their bodies and hold negative beliefs about their appearance. This can lead to feelings of dissatisfaction, low self-esteem, and anxiety about one's body. Overcoming negative body image is an important process that involves challenging and changing these negative thoughts and beliefs in order to develop a healthier and more positive view of oneself. In this discussion, we will explore the factors that contribute to negative body image, the potential consequences of holding on to these beliefs, and strategies for overcoming negative body image and cultivating self-acceptance and self-confidence.

There are a variety of factors that can contribute to the development of negative body image. Society plays a significant role in shaping the way we perceive our bodies, with media, advertising, and social media platforms often portraying narrow and unrealistic beauty standards that can leave individuals feeling inadequate and dissatisfied with their own appearance. In addition, personal experiences such as teasing, bullying, or interpersonal conflicts can also contribute to a negative body image. Furthermore, genetic and biological factors, as well as mental health conditions such as depression and anxiety, can also impact how individuals perceive themselves. It is important to recognize that negative body image is a complex issue that can be influenced by a combination of internal and external factors.

The consequences of holding on to negative body image beliefs can be far-reaching and have a significant impact on an individual's mental and emotional well-being. Research has shown that individuals with negative body image are more likely to experience symptoms of depression, anxiety, and low self-esteem. They may also engage in harmful behaviors such as disordered eating, excessive exercise, or substance abuse in an attempt to change their appearance and feel better about themselves. This can create a vicious cycle of negative thoughts and behaviors that can further exacerbate feelings of dissatisfaction and discontent with one's body. Over time, the persistent focus on perceived flaws and imperfections can erode self-worth and prevent individuals from fully engaging in and enjoying their lives.

Overcoming negative body image requires a multifaceted approach that addresses both the internal beliefs and external influences that contribute to these negative perceptions. One important step in this process is to challenge and reframe negative thoughts and beliefs about one's appearance. This may involve identifying and challenging cognitive distortions, such as all-or-nothing thinking or magnifying perceived flaws, and replacing them with more balanced and realistic perspectives. Additionally, practicing self-compassion and acceptance can help individuals learn to appreciate and respect their bodies for all that they do and provide, rather than focusing solely on appearance-based criteria.

In addition to changing internal beliefs, it is also important to address external factors that contribute to negative body image. This may involve limiting exposure to media and advertising that promote unrealistic beauty standards, surrounding oneself with supportive and affirming individuals, and seeking out positive sources of inspiration and empowerment. Engaging in activities that promote self-care, such as exercise, mindfulness, or creative expression, can also help individuals reconnect with their bodies and develop a more positive relationship with themselves. By creating a supportive and nurturing environment, individuals can begin to cultivate self-acceptance and self-love that extends beyond physical appearance. By recognizing and challenging negative beliefs, addressing external influences, and practicing self-care and self-compassion, individuals can begin to shift their focus from perceived flaws and imperfections to their inherent worth and value as human beings. Through this process, individuals can learn to embrace their bodies and appreciate all that they have to offer, leading to a more positive and fulfilling relationship with themselves and the world around them.

- Building self-compassion through mindfulness

In recent years, mindfulness has gained significant attention as a powerful tool for building self-compassion. Self-compassion, as defined by psychologist Kristin Neff, involves treating oneself with the same kindness, care, and understanding that one would offer to a close friend in times of suffering or failure. It encompasses three key components: self-kindness, common humanity, and mindfulness. While self-compassion may not come naturally to everyone, research has shown that mindfulness practices can help individuals develop this crucial skill.

Mindfulness, at its core, involves being fully present and engaged in the current moment without judgment. By cultivating mindfulness, individuals can develop a deeper awareness of their thoughts, feelings, and sensations, allowing them to respond to themselves with greater kindness and care. This heightened sense of self-awareness enables individuals to recognize when they are being self-critical or judgmental and to consciously choose to respond with self-compassion instead.

One of the key ways in which mindfulness helps build self-compassion is by fostering a sense of common humanity. When individuals are able to recognize that suffering and imperfection are universal human experiences, they are less likely to feel isolated or alone in their struggles. Mindfulness practices, such as meditation and mindful breathing, help individuals connect with this sense of common humanity by focusing on the present moment and acknowledging their own vulnerabilities and limitations.

Furthermore, mindfulness encourages individuals to approach their thoughts and feelings with curiosity and nonjudgmental acceptance. This open-hearted attitude allows individuals to observe their inner experiences without getting caught up in self-criticism or self-blame. By cultivating a nonjudgmental stance toward their thoughts and emotions, individuals can create a safe and compassionate space within themselves to acknowledge and validate their own suffering.

In addition to fostering self-compassion through common humanity and nonjudgmental acceptance, mindfulness practices also help individuals develop self-kindness. By paying attention to their inner experiences and responding to themselves with kindness and care, individuals can learn to be more nurturing and supportive toward themselves in times of difficulty or distress. Through mindfulness practices, individuals can cultivate a sense of self-worth and self-acceptance that lays the foundation for self-compassion.

One of the key mindfulness practices that can help individuals build self-compassion is loving-kindness meditation. This practice involves silently repeating phrases of goodwill and compassion toward oneself and others. By engaging in loving-kindness meditation regularly, individuals can cultivate feelings of warmth, acceptance, and kindness toward themselves, ultimately fostering a greater sense of self-compassion.

Another valuable mindfulness practice for building self-compassion is self-compassion meditation. This practice involves guiding individuals through a series of compassionate phrases and imagery to help them develop a sense of self-compassion and understanding. Through self-compassion meditation, individuals can learn to respond to their own suffering with kindness and care, ultimately strengthening their ability to be self-compassionate in their daily lives. By cultivating a sense of common humanity, nonjudgmental acceptance, and self-kindness through mindfulness practices, individuals can learn to respond to themselves with the same kindness and care that they would offer to a close friend. Through practices such as loving-kindness meditation and self-compassion meditation, individuals can develop a deeper sense of self-compassion and cultivate a greater sense of well-being and resilience in their lives.

Chapter 9: Letting Go of Stress

- RECOGNIZING AND RELEASING stress

Stress is a common phenomenon that affects individuals in various aspects of their lives. It is essential to recognize the signs and symptoms of stress to effectively manage and release it. Recognizing stress involves being aware of physical, emotional, and behavioral changes that may indicate a high level of stress. These changes may include increased heart rate, muscle tension, fatigue, irritability, and changes in appetite or sleep patterns. Being attuned to these signs allows individuals to take proactive steps to address the underlying causes of stress and prevent it from escalating.

Once stress is recognized, it is crucial to release it in a healthy and constructive manner. There are various strategies that individuals can employ to manage and release stress effectively. One common approach is mindfulness meditation, which involves focusing on the present moment and observing thoughts and feelings without judgment. This practice can help individuals cultivate a sense of calm and reduce stress levels. Physical exercise is another effective way to release stress, as it releases endorphins and promotes relaxation. Engaging in activities such as yoga, jogging, or dancing can help individuals channel their stress into physical movement and release built-up tension.

In addition to mindfulness meditation and physical exercise, individuals can also employ relaxation techniques such as deep breathing exercises, progressive muscle relaxation, or visualization. These techniques can help individuals relax their bodies and minds, promoting a sense of tranquility and reducing stress levels. It is essential for individuals to find the relaxation technique that works best for them and to incorporate it into their daily routine to manage stress effectively. Setting aside time each day for relaxation and self-care can help individuals maintain a healthy balance and release stress in a sustainable manner.

Furthermore, it is important for individuals to identify and address the underlying causes of their stress to prevent it from recurring. Common sources of stress may include work-related pressures, relationship issues, financial concerns, or health problems. By identifying these triggers, individuals can take proactive steps to address them and reduce their impact on their overall well-being. This may involve setting boundaries at work, improving communication in relationships, seeking financial advice, or seeking professional help for health issues. By taking proactive steps to address the root causes of stress, individuals can prevent it from escalating and maintain a healthy balance in their lives. By being attuned to the signs and symptoms of stress, individuals can take proactive steps to manage it effectively. Engaging in mindfulness meditation, physical exercise, relaxation techniques, and addressing the underlying causes of stress can help individuals release tension and maintain a healthy balance in their lives. It is important for individuals to prioritize self-care and make time for relaxation to prevent stress from escalating. By incorporating these strategies into their daily routine, individuals can effectively manage stress and promote their overall well-being.

- Coping with stress through mindfulness

Stress is an inevitable part of life that most individuals will encounter at some point. It can stem from various sources such as work, relationships, health issues, or even societal pressures. When left unchecked, stress can have detrimental effects on both mental and physical well-being. Fortunately, there are coping mechanisms that can help individuals manage and alleviate stress. One such method is mindfulness, which has gained popularity in recent years for its effectiveness in reducing stress and promoting overall well-being.

Mindfulness is the practice of being fully present and aware of one's thoughts, feelings, bodily sensations, and surrounding environment. It involves paying attention to the present moment without judgment or attachment. Mindfulness allows individuals to acknowledge their thoughts and emotions without becoming overwhelmed by them. By cultivating mindfulness, individuals can develop a greater sense of control over their reactions to stressors and ultimately reduce their overall stress levels.

One of the key components of mindfulness is awareness of the breath. Breathing exercises are a common mindfulness practice that can help individuals ground themselves in the present moment and alleviate feelings of stress and anxiety. By focusing on the breath, individuals can slow down racing thoughts and calm their nervous system. Deep breathing exercises can also help individuals release physical tension in the body, which is often a physical manifestation of stress.

In addition to breathing exercises, mindfulness meditation is another effective tool for coping with stress. Meditation involves sitting quietly and focusing the mind on a specific object, such as the breath or a mantra. Through regular meditation practice, individuals can train their minds to be more present and aware, which can enhance their ability to cope with stress. Research has shown that mindfulness meditation can reduce levels of cortisol, the stress hormone, and promote feelings of relaxation and well-being.

Another aspect of mindfulness that can help individuals cope with stress is acceptance. Acceptance involves acknowledging and embracing one's thoughts and emotions without trying to change or suppress them. By accepting their thoughts and feelings, individuals can create a sense of inner peace and reduce the internal struggle that often accompanies stress. Mindfulness teaches individuals to let go of the need to control every aspect of their lives and instead embrace the uncertainty and impermanence of the present moment.

Mindfulness can also help individuals develop a sense of gratitude and appreciation for the small moments in life. By focusing on the present moment and cultivating a sense of gratitude, individuals can shift their perspective from one of stress and negativity to one of positivity and appreciation. Gratitude practices, such as keeping a gratitude journal or engaging in acts of kindness, can help individuals reframe their mindset and cope with stress in a more positive and resilient manner. By cultivating a sense of awareness, acceptance, and gratitude, individuals can develop a greater sense of control over their reactions to stressors and reduce their overall stress levels. Breathing exercises, mindfulness meditation, acceptance, and gratitude practices are just a few of the ways that individuals can incorporate mindfulness into their daily lives to cope with stress. With consistent practice and dedication, mindfulness can help individuals navigate the challenges of stress and cultivate a greater sense of peace and well-being.

- Creating a calm and centered mindset

Creating a calm and centered mindset is essential for maintaining overall well-being and living a balanced and fulfilling life. In today's fast-paced world, it is easy to get caught up in stress, anxiety, and distractions that can negatively impact our mental and emotional state. By cultivating a calm and centered mindset, we can better navigate challenges, make decisions with clarity, and enjoy a greater sense of peace and contentment.

One of the key aspects of creating a calm and centered mindset is developing a consistent mindfulness practice. Mindfulness involves being fully present in the moment, paying attention to our thoughts and feelings without judgment. This practice can help us become more aware of our internal state and external surroundings, which can lead to a greater sense of calm and clarity. Taking time each day to practice mindfulness through meditation, deep breathing exercises, or simply being present in the moment can help us cultivate a sense of inner peace and balance.

In addition to mindfulness, another important aspect of creating a calm and centered mindset is learning to manage stress effectively. Stress is a natural part of life, but when left unchecked, it can have a negative impact on our mental and physical health. By developing healthy coping mechanisms for stress, such as exercise, relaxation techniques, or seeking support from others, we can better manage our stress levels and prevent it from overwhelming us. It is also important to prioritize self-care and make time for activities that bring us joy and relaxation, such as spending time in nature, practicing yoga, or engaging in creative hobbies.

Another important aspect of creating a calm and centered mindset is cultivating a positive and balanced perspective on life. This involves practicing gratitude, focusing on the present moment, and letting go of negative thoughts and emotions. By adopting a mindset of gratitude and appreciation, we can shift our focus from what is lacking in our lives to what we have to be thankful for. This can help us cultivate a sense of contentment and peace, even in the face of challenges and difficulties. Additionally, focusing on the present moment and letting go of worries about the past or future can help us maintain a sense of calm and centeredness.

It is also important to cultivate a sense of self-awareness and self-compassion in order to create a calm and centered mindset. Self-awareness involves understanding our own thoughts, feelings, and behaviors, and being able to identify when we are experiencing stress or negative emotions. By cultivating self-awareness, we can better understand our triggers and learn to respond to challenging situations in a more mindful and compassionate way. Practicing self-compassion involves treating ourselves with kindness and understanding, especially when we are facing difficulties or setbacks. By being gentle with ourselves and practicing self-compassion, we can cultivate a sense of calm and centeredness even in the midst of chaos and uncertainty. By developing a consistent mindfulness practice, learning to manage stress effectively, cultivating a positive and balanced perspective on life, and practicing self-awareness and self-compassion, we can cultivate a sense of inner peace and balance. By incorporating these practices into our daily routine, we can better navigate challenges, make decisions with clarity, and enjoy a greater sense of peace and contentment. Ultimately, by prioritizing our mental and emotional well-being, we can live a more fulfilling and meaningful life.

Chapter 10: Gratitude Meditation

- CULTIVATING APPRECIATION and gratitude

Cultivating appreciation and gratitude is a transformative practice that can bring countless benefits to one's life. By focusing on the positive aspects of our experiences and relationships, we can shift our perspective to one of abundance and thankfulness. This shift in mindset has been shown to have a multitude of positive effects on both our mental and physical well-being.

One of the key components of cultivating gratitude is simply taking the time to acknowledge and reflect on the things we are grateful for. This can be done through journaling, meditation, or simply taking a few moments each day to think about the blessings in our lives. By making a conscious effort to focus on the positive, we can begin to rewire our brains to naturally seek out and appreciate the good in our lives.

In addition to the immediate emotional benefits of gratitude, research has shown that practicing gratitude can have long-lasting effects on our mental health. Studies have found that individuals who regularly practice gratitude are more likely to experience lower levels of depression and anxiety, as well as higher levels of overall life satisfaction. By fostering a sense of appreciation for the people, things, and experiences that bring us joy, we can create a buffer against the stresses and challenges of everyday life.

Cultivating gratitude can also have a profound impact on our relationships with others. When we take the time to express our appreciation for those around us, it can strengthen our connections and foster a sense of closeness and trust. By showing gratitude towards others, we not only uplift their spirits but also create a positive feedback loop that can lead to even more opportunities for connection and collaboration.

Furthermore, the practice of gratitude can help us to cultivate a greater sense of resilience in the face of adversity. By focusing on the things we are grateful for, we can develop a more positive outlook on life and a greater sense of hope and optimism. This can help us to navigate challenges with a greater sense of grace and fortitude, knowing that we have a reservoir of positivity to draw upon.

There are many different ways to cultivate gratitude in our lives, and it is important to find a practice that resonates with us personally. Some people may find that keeping a gratitude journal or practicing daily affirmations is most effective for them, while others may prefer to express their gratitude through acts of kindness and service to others. Whatever form it takes, the key is to make gratitude a regular part of our daily routine, so that it becomes a natural and integral aspect of our mindset. By focusing on the positive aspects of our experiences and relationships, we can shift our perspective to one of abundance and thankfulness. This can have a profound impact on our mental and physical well-being, as well as our relationships with others. By making gratitude a regular part of our daily routine, we can create a more positive and resilient mindset that can help us navigate the challenges of life with grace and courage.

- Shifting focus to positivity

In recent years, there has been a notable shift in focus towards positivity in various aspects of life, including psychology, business, and personal development. This shift towards positivity emphasizes the importance of focusing on strengths, virtues, and solutions rather than dwelling on problems and shortcomings. This approach has gained popularity due to its numerous benefits, including improved mental health, increased productivity, and enhanced overall well-being.

One of the key principles of shifting focus to positivity is the concept of positive psychology. Positive psychology is a branch of psychology that focuses on positive emotions, strengths, and virtues, rather than solely on treating mental illness or dysfunction. This field of psychology aims to help individuals flourish and thrive by identifying and utilizing their strengths and positive qualities. By focusing on positivity in therapy and counseling sessions, therapists can help clients build resilience, enhance their self-esteem, and cultivate a positive mindset.

In the business world, the shift towards positivity is evident in the growing popularity of positive leadership and positive organizational behavior. Positive leadership involves leading with a focus on strengths, encouragement, and optimism, rather than relying on fear, criticism, or punishment. Positive leaders inspire their teams to perform at their best, foster a culture of collaboration and innovation, and create a positive work environment where employees feel valued and motivated. Positive organizational behavior, on the other hand, focuses on fostering positive emotions, attitudes, and behaviors within organizations. By cultivating a positive work culture, organizations can improve employee engagement, job satisfaction, and overall performance.

On a personal level, shifting focus to positivity can have profound effects on one's mental health and well-being. Research has shown that practicing gratitude, optimism, and mindfulness can lead to improved mood, reduced anxiety and depression, and increased overall life satisfaction. By focusing on positive thoughts and emotions, individuals can reframe negative situations, build resilience, and cultivate a sense of inner peace and contentment. Additionally, practicing positivity can enhance relationships, boost self-confidence, and promote personal growth and development.

Despite the numerous benefits of shifting focus to positivity, it is important to acknowledge that it is not about denying or ignoring challenges, difficulties, or negative emotions. Instead, it is about learning to approach these challenges with a positive mindset, seeking out opportunities for growth and learning, and finding ways to cultivate joy and gratitude in the face of adversity. By shifting focus to positivity, individuals can build emotional resilience, foster stronger relationships, and enhance their overall well-being. Ultimately, the key to embracing positivity lies in adopting a growth mindset, practicing self-compassion, and cultivating an attitude of gratitude and optimism in all aspects of life.

- Enhancing overall well-being through gratitude

Enhancing overall well-being through gratitude is a widely researched and well-documented concept in the field of positive psychology. Gratitude, defined as the feeling of thankfulness and appreciation, has been shown to have numerous benefits for individuals' mental, emotional, and physical well-being. By cultivating a practice of gratitude, individuals can experience increased happiness, improved relationships, better physical health, and a greater sense of meaning and purpose in life.

One of the key ways in which gratitude enhances overall well-being is by shifting individuals' focus from what they lack to what they have. In our fast-paced and consumer-driven society, it is easy to become caught up in a mindset of scarcity and comparison, constantly striving for more and feeling dissatisfied with what we already have. Cultivating gratitude helps us to stop and appreciate the blessings and abundance in our lives, whether big or small. Research has shown that individuals who regularly practice gratitude are more likely to experience positive emotions such as joy, contentment, and optimism, leading to a greater sense of overall well-being.

In addition to increasing positive emotions, gratitude has also been linked to improved mental health outcomes. Studies have found that individuals who practice gratitude have lower levels of depression and anxiety, as well as higher levels of self-esteem and resilience. By focusing on what they are grateful for, individuals are able to reframe negative situations in a more positive light, leading to a greater sense of hope and perspective. Gratitude also fosters a sense of connection and social support, as individuals who express gratitude are more likely to build and maintain strong relationships with others. This in turn can lead to increased feelings of belonging and acceptance, further enhancing overall well-being.

Furthermore, gratitude has been shown to have physical health benefits as well. Research has found that individuals who practice gratitude have lower levels of stress, better sleep quality, and stronger immune systems. By focusing on the positive aspects of their lives, individuals are able to reduce stress and anxiety levels, leading to improved physical health outcomes. Gratitude has also been linked to lower levels of inflammation in the body, which can help protect against chronic diseases such as heart disease and diabetes. By practicing gratitude on a regular basis, individuals can improve their overall well-being by taking care of both their mental and physical health.

In order to enhance overall well-being through gratitude, there are a variety of strategies that individuals can use to cultivate a sense of thankfulness and appreciation in their lives. One simple but effective strategy is to keep a gratitude journal, where individuals can write down three things they are grateful for each day. This practice helps to train the brain to focus on the positive aspects of life, leading to an increased sense of well-being over time. Another strategy is to express gratitude to others, whether through words of thanks, acts of kindness, or small gestures of appreciation. By showing gratitude to those around us, we not only strengthen our relationships but also increase our own sense of well-being. By cultivating a sense of thankfulness and appreciation, individuals can experience increased happiness, improved relationships, better physical health, and a greater sense of meaning and purpose in life. Gratitude helps to shift individuals' focus from what they lack to what they have, leading to a greater sense of abundance and contentment. By practicing gratitude on a regular basis, individuals can reap the numerous benefits of this simple but transformative practice.

Chapter 11: Mindful Communication

- IMPROVING RELATIONSHIPS through mindful communication

In today's fast-paced world, effective communication is more critical than ever in fostering strong and healthy relationships. Mindful communication, a practice rooted in mindfulness and compassion, offers a mindful approach to communicating with others that can improve relationships both personally and professionally. By cultivating awareness of our thoughts, feelings, and intentions, we can better understand others and express ourselves more clearly and authentically. Mindful communication involves active listening, acknowledging emotions, and responding with empathy and kindness. In this way, it promotes deeper connections and greater understanding between individuals, leading to stronger and more fulfilling relationships.

One of the key principles of mindful communication is the practice of active listening. This involves giving our full attention to the speaker, without judgment or distraction. By truly listening to what others have to say, we can better understand their perspective, feelings, and needs. Active listening requires us to be fully present in the moment, setting aside our own biases and assumptions to focus on the speaker's words and emotions. This kind of attentive listening fosters trust and respect in relationships, as it shows that we value and care about the other person's thoughts and feelings.

In addition to active listening, mindful communication involves acknowledging emotions, both our own and those of others. Emotions play a significant role in communication, influencing how we perceive and respond to each other. By becoming more aware of our own emotions and how they affect our communication, we can better regulate our reactions and avoid unnecessary conflicts. Similarly, by recognizing and validating the emotions of others, we show empathy and understanding, creating a more supportive and empathetic relationship. This emotional awareness allows for more honest and constructive conversations, as it encourages a deeper level of trust and mutual respect.

Furthermore, mindful communication emphasizes responding with empathy and kindness. This means considering the impact of our words and actions on others and choosing to communicate in a way that is compassionate and respectful. By acknowledging the humanity and inherent worth of every individual, we can create an atmosphere of trust and understanding in our relationships. Responding with empathy means taking the time to consider the feelings and needs of others before speaking or acting, and choosing words that are thoughtful and supportive. This kind of compassionate communication builds strong and lasting connections, based on mutual respect and care. By cultivating awareness, empathy, and kindness in our interactions with others, we can create stronger connections, resolve conflicts more effectively, and build more fulfilling relationships. Mindful communication allows us to communicate authentically, from a place of genuine understanding and compassion, fostering deeper connections and mutual respect. In today's fast-paced and often chaotic world, taking the time to communicate mindfully can have a profound impact on our relationships, promoting harmony, understanding, and collaboration in all aspects of our lives.

- Listening with empathy and presence

Listening with empathy and presence plays a crucial role in effective communication and fostering positive relationships. It requires not only hearing the words spoken by another person but also understanding and connecting with their emotions, perspectives, and experiences. Empathy involves putting yourself in someone else's shoes and showing genuine care and concern for their feelings. Presence, on the other hand, means being fully engaged in the moment and giving your undivided attention to the speaker. By combining empathy and presence, you can create a safe and supportive environment where people feel heard, valued, and understood.

When we listen with empathy and presence, we validate the other person's thoughts and feelings, which can have a powerful impact on their well-being.

By acknowledging and accepting their emotions, we show respect and compassion, and we help them feel less alone in their struggles. This sense of validation can be particularly important in difficult or emotional situations when someone is going through a challenging time and needs to feel heard and supported. Without empathy and presence, our interactions can feel superficial and disconnected, leaving the other person feeling misunderstood or dismissed.

In addition to providing emotional support, listening with empathy and presence can also enhance our understanding of different perspectives and experiences. When we approach conversations with an open mind and a willingness to truly listen, we can learn a great deal from others and broaden our own perspectives. By practicing empathy and presence, we can build trust and rapport with those around us, creating a sense of mutual respect and understanding that can lead to deeper and more meaningful relationships. This ability to connect with others on a deeper level can enrich our personal and professional lives and open up new opportunities for growth and development.

Empathy and presence are not just about the words we say or the actions we take; they are also about the energy and attitude we bring to our interactions. When we approach conversations with a genuine desire to understand and connect with others, we can create a sense of trust and openness that allows for more meaningful communication. By paying attention to both verbal and nonverbal cues, such as body language, tone of voice, and facial expressions, we can gain a deeper insight into the emotions and intentions of the speaker. This awareness can help us respond more effectively and create a more supportive and empathetic environment for meaningful dialogue.

In order to cultivate empathy and presence in our interactions, it is important to practice active listening, which involves giving our full attention to the speaker and showing that we are engaged and interested in what they have to say. This means avoiding distractions, such as checking our phones or thinking about what we will say next, and focusing on the speaker's words and emotions. By actively listening, we can demonstrate our empathy and presence by showing that we value and respect the other person's perspective and that we are committed to understanding and supporting them.

In addition to active listening, it is also important to practice reflective listening, which involves paraphrasing and summarizing the speaker's words to ensure that we have understood their message correctly. By reflecting back what we have heard, we can demonstrate our empathy and presence by showing that we are paying attention and that we care about the speaker's thoughts and feelings. This can help clarify any misunderstandings and ensure that both parties are on the same page, leading to more effective communication and a deeper connection.

It is also important to be mindful of our own biases and assumptions when listening to others. We all bring our own experiences, beliefs, and perspectives to the table, which can influence how we interpret and respond to what others say. By being aware of our biases and practicing empathy and presence, we can avoid jumping to conclusions or making assumptions about the speaker's intentions. Instead, we can approach conversations with an open mind and a willingness to learn from others, allowing for more meaningful and productive dialogue.

Ultimately, listening with empathy and presence is a skill that requires practice and intentionality. By cultivating empathy and presence in our interactions, we can create a more supportive and understanding environment for meaningful communication and connection. Whether in personal or professional settings, the ability to listen with empathy and presence can foster positive relationships, enhance our understanding of others, and lead to more effective communication and collaboration. By making a conscious effort to approach conversations with empathy and presence, we can build stronger connections with those around us and create a more inclusive and supportive community.

- Resolving conflicts mindfully

Conflicts are an inevitable part of human interaction, occurring in various contexts such as workplaces, friendships, families, and romantic relationships. While conflict itself is not inherently negative, as it can lead to growth, it can also result in stress, tension, and damaged relationships if not managed effectively. Resolving conflicts mindfully is an approach that emphasizes self-awareness, empathy, and communication skills to address disagreements in a constructive and respectful manner.

Mindful conflict resolution involves being present in the moment and fully engaging with the conflict without judgment or bias. This requires individuals to cultivate self-awareness and emotional intelligence, recognizing their own triggers, biases, and emotional reactions that may fuel the conflict. By acknowledging and understanding their own emotions and perspectives, individuals can approach the conflict with a calmer and more rational mindset, making it easier to communicate effectively and reach a resolution that is mutually beneficial.

In addition to self-awareness, mindful conflict resolution also emphasizes empathy towards the other party involved in the conflict. This involves putting oneself in the other person's shoes, trying to understand their perspectives, needs, and emotions. By practicing empathy, individuals can foster a sense of compassion and understanding towards the other person, which can help de-escalate the conflict and create a more collaborative environment for resolution.

Effective communication is another key element of mindful conflict resolution. This involves active listening, speaking honestly and respectfully, and expressing one's needs and concerns clearly. By maintaining open and honest communication, individuals can avoid misunderstandings, clarify expectations, and work towards finding common ground and solutions to the conflict. It is important to use "I" statements rather than "you" statements to avoid blame and defensiveness, and to focus on expressing feelings and needs rather than making accusations or criticism.

Conflict resolution requires a willingness to compromise and find win-win solutions that address the needs of both parties involved. This may involve brainstorming creative solutions, seeking feedback from others, and being open to alternative perspectives. By being flexible and open-minded, individuals can explore different options and find a resolution that is satisfactory to all parties.

Mindful conflict resolution also involves managing emotions effectively during the conflict. This includes learning how to regulate emotions, practice patience, and use mindfulness techniques such as deep breathing or meditation to stay calm and focused in challenging situations. By remaining composed and level-headed, individuals can avoid escalating the conflict and find a more constructive way to address the issues at hand. By approaching conflicts with mindfulness and compassion, individuals can navigate disagreements in a constructive and respectful manner, leading to stronger relationships, improved communication, and a deeper understanding of themselves and others. By practicing mindful conflict resolution, individuals can transform conflicts into opportunities for growth, learning, and positive change in their personal and professional lives.

Chapter 12: Sleep Meditation

- TECHNIQUES FOR RELAXING the mind before sleep

Fortunately, there are a variety of techniques that can help us relax our minds and bodies before sleep, promoting a restful and rejuvenating night's rest.

One highly effective technique for relaxing the mind before sleep is progressive muscle relaxation. This technique involves systematically tensing and then relaxing each muscle group in the body, starting from the toes and working up to the head. By intentionally tensing and then releasing the muscles, we can help to release physical tension and promote a state of relaxation. This process can help to quiet the mind and reduce anxiety, making it easier to drift off to sleep.

Another technique that can help to relax the mind before sleep is deep breathing exercises. Deep breathing can help to calm the nervous system and reduce the body's stress response, promoting feelings of relaxation and tranquility. To practice deep breathing, simply find a comfortable position, close your eyes, and take slow, deep breaths in through the nose and out through the mouth. Focus on each breath as it enters and exits your body, allowing yourself to let go of any racing thoughts or worries.

Mindfulness meditation is another powerful technique for calming the mind before sleep. Mindfulness involves being fully present in the moment, without judgment or distraction. By focusing on the sensations of the breath or the sounds around you, you can cultivate a sense of inner calm and quiet the chatter of the mind. Practicing mindfulness meditation before bed can help to create a sense of peace and relaxation, making it easier to transition into a restful sleep.

Guided imagery is another helpful technique for relaxing the mind before sleep. Guided imagery involves visualizing a peaceful and calming scene, such as a serene beach or a tranquil forest. By picturing yourself in this calming environment, you can help to soothe the mind and reduce feelings of stress and anxiety. Many people find that guided imagery can be a helpful tool for promoting relaxation before bedtime, allowing them to drift off to sleep more easily.

Listening to calming music or nature sounds can also be a helpful technique for relaxing the mind before sleep. Music has the power to influence our emotions and mood, and listening to calming music before bed can help to create a soothing and peaceful atmosphere. Nature sounds, such as the sound of ocean waves or a gentle rain shower, can also have a calming effect on the mind and body. By incorporating soothing sounds into your bedtime routine, you can help to create a relaxing environment that promotes restful sleep.

In addition to these techniques, creating a bedtime routine can also help to relax the mind before sleep. Establishing a consistent routine can signal to the body that it is time to wind down and prepare for rest. This can include activities such as reading a book, taking a warm bath, or practicing gentle stretching exercises. By following a consistent bedtime routine, you can help to create a sense of structure and predictability that can promote relaxation and restful sleep. By practicing progressive muscle relaxation, deep breathing exercises, mindfulness meditation, guided imagery, listening to calming music or nature sounds, and establishing a bedtime routine, you can create a peaceful and calming environment that promotes relaxation and restful sleep.

- Enhancing sleep quality through mindfulness

In today's fast-paced and often stressful world, factors such as work pressures, electronic devices, and busy schedules can all contribute to poor sleep quality. Fortunately, there are various strategies that can help improve the quality of our sleep, one of which is mindfulness.

Mindfulness is a practice that involves being fully present and aware in the moment, without judgment or attachment to thoughts or feelings. When it comes to sleep, mindfulness can be a powerful tool to help calm the mind, relax the body, and create the conditions for restful sleep.

One way that mindfulness can enhance sleep quality is by helping to reduce the racing thoughts and worries that often keep us awake at night. By practicing mindfulness techniques such as deep breathing, body scan, or meditation before bed, we can quiet the mind and cultivate a sense of calm and relaxation that is conducive to falling asleep. Mindfulness can also help us to let go of the day's stresses and anxieties, allowing us to fully unwind and prepare for rest.

In addition to calming the mind, mindfulness can also help us to tune into the body and become more aware of physical sensations that may be affecting our sleep. For example, by practicing body scan meditation, we can gently scan through the body, noticing any areas of tension or discomfort and releasing them through deep breathing and relaxation. This can help to reduce physical symptoms such as muscle tension or pain that may be interfering with our ability to fall or stay asleep.

Another way that mindfulness can enhance sleep quality is by promoting a sense of acceptance and non-judgment towards our sleep patterns. Many of us have high expectations and pressures around sleep, leading to frustration and anxiety when we struggle to fall or stay asleep. By practicing mindfulness, we can learn to approach our sleep with a gentle and compassionate attitude, letting go of the need to control or fix our sleep and instead, simply allowing it to unfold naturally.

Moreover, mindfulness can also help us to establish healthy bedtime routines and habits that support restful sleep. By incorporating mindfulness practices into our evening rituals, such as dimming the lights, turning off electronic devices, and practicing relaxation techniques, we can signal to our bodies that it is time for sleep and create a conducive environment for rest. By cultivating a sense of mindfulness and presence in our nighttime routine, we can set the stage for a peaceful and rejuvenating night's sleep. By practicing mindfulness techniques such as deep breathing, body scan, and meditation before bed, we can calm the mind, relax the body, and create the conditions for restful sleep. Mindfulness can also help us to tune into physical sensations, release tension and discomfort, and establish healthy bedtime routines that support restful sleep. By cultivating a sense of acceptance, compassion, and presence towards our sleep, we can let go of anxiety and expectations, and instead, approach sleep with a gentle and open-hearted attitude.

- Finding restful and rejuvenating sleep

Sleep is a fundamental aspect of human existence, essential for our physical and mental well-being. A restful and rejuvenating night's sleep is crucial for maintaining optimal health and function. However, with the demands of modern life, many people struggle to achieve the quality and quantity of sleep necessary for optimal health. In this article, we will explore the importance of restful and rejuvenating sleep, the factors that can impact our ability to achieve it, and strategies for improving our sleep quality.

The benefits of restful and rejuvenating sleep are numerous and far-reaching. During sleep, the body undergoes essential processes that support overall health and well-being. These processes include the repair and regeneration of tissues, the consolidation of memories, and the regulation of hormones that govern appetite, mood, and stress. Inadequate sleep can have a detrimental impact on these processes, leading to cognitive impairments, mood disturbances, and an increased risk of chronic health conditions such as obesity, diabetes, and cardiovascular disease.

There are several factors that can affect our ability to achieve restful and rejuvenating sleep. One of the most common culprits is poor sleep hygiene, which refers to the habits and practices that can either promote or hinder the quality of our sleep. These can include excessive screen time before bed, consuming caffeine or alcohol close to bedtime, and sleeping in an uncomfortable or unsupportive environment. Other factors that can impact our sleep quality include stress, underlying health conditions, and certain medications.

Fortunately, there are steps we can take to improve our sleep hygiene and promote restful and rejuvenating sleep. One of the most important strategies is to establish a consistent sleep routine, going to bed and waking up at the same time each day, even on weekends. This can help regulate our body's internal clock, known as the circadian rhythm, and improve the quality of our sleep. Additionally, creating a calming bedtime routine can signal to our bodies that it is time to wind down and prepare for sleep. This can include activities such as reading, meditating, or taking a warm bath.

Creating a sleep-conducive environment is also key to achieving restful and rejuvenating sleep. This can involve keeping your bedroom cool, dark, and quiet, as well as investing in a comfortable mattress and pillows that support your body's natural alignment. It is also important to limit exposure to screens and artificial light before bed, as these can interfere with the production of melatonin, a hormone that regulates our sleep-wake cycle.

In addition to improving sleep hygiene, there are other strategies that can help promote restful and rejuvenating sleep. Regular physical activity has been shown to improve sleep quality, as it can reduce stress and anxiety, two common culprits of poor sleep. In addition, practicing relaxation techniques such as deep breathing, progressive muscle relaxation, or mindfulness meditation can help calm the mind and prepare the body for sleep. To sum up, if you continue to struggle with sleep despite making these changes, it may be helpful to consult with a healthcare professional or sleep specialist to rule out underlying sleep disorders or other health conditions. By prioritizing good sleep hygiene, creating a sleep-conducive environment, and implementing strategies to reduce stress and promote relaxation, you can improve the quality and quantity of your sleep. Remember that sleep is not a luxury but a necessity, and investing in your rest can have profound benefits for your physical, mental, and emotional health. By making sleep a priority in your life, you can wake up feeling refreshed, energized, and ready to take on the day.

Chapter 13: Dealing with Anxiety

- RECOGNIZING AND MANAGING anxiety symptoms

Anxiety is a common emotional response to stress and can manifest in various ways. It is essential to recognize and manage anxiety symptoms to improve overall well-being and quality of life. Understanding the signs of anxiety can help individuals seek appropriate support and treatment to alleviate distress and prevent further complications.

Recognizing anxiety symptoms can be complex as they can present differently in each individual. Common physical manifestations of anxiety may include rapid heartbeat, sweating, trembling, and shortness of breath. These physical symptoms are often accompanied by psychological signs such as excessive worry, irritability, difficulty concentrating, and feelings of dread or impending doom. Behavioral manifestations of anxiety can include avoidance of certain situations, restlessness, excessive use of alcohol or drugs, and changes in appetite or sleep patterns. It is important to be mindful of these symptoms as they can significantly impact daily functioning and overall well-being.

Managing anxiety symptoms involves a multi-faceted approach that can include lifestyle changes, therapy, and medication. One of the first steps in managing anxiety is to identify triggers that may be exacerbating symptoms. Keeping a journal to track thoughts, emotions, and behaviors can help individuals recognize patterns and develop coping strategies. Engaging in regular exercise, practicing relaxation techniques such as deep breathing or meditation, and maintaining a healthy diet can also help reduce anxiety symptoms. Additionally, seeking support from friends, family, or a therapist can offer a safe space to explore feelings and learn new ways to manage anxiety.

Cognitive-behavioral therapy (CBT) is a widely used therapeutic approach for managing anxiety symptoms. CBT helps individuals identify and challenge negative thought patterns that contribute to anxiety and teaches coping strategies to change unhelpful behaviors. Through CBT, individuals can learn skills to manage stress and anxiety in a more adaptive way, ultimately improving their ability to cope with life's challenges. In some cases, medication may be prescribed to help alleviate severe anxiety symptoms. It is important to work closely with a healthcare provider to determine the most appropriate treatment plan based on individual needs and preferences.

In addition to individual therapy, group therapy and support groups can also be beneficial for managing anxiety symptoms. Connecting with others who are experiencing similar challenges can provide a sense of community and understanding. Group therapy allows individuals to share experiences, learn from others, and receive encouragement and support from peers. Support groups can also provide a safe space to discuss feelings, share coping strategies, and reduce feelings of isolation that often accompany anxiety.

Self-care practices can play a significant role in managing anxiety symptoms and promoting overall well-being. Engaging in activities that bring joy and relaxation, such as hobbies, exercise, or spending time in nature, can help reduce stress and alleviate anxiety. Practicing mindfulness and self-compassion can also be beneficial in cultivating a sense of calm and resilience. It is important to prioritize self-care and make time for activities that nourish the mind, body, and soul. By understanding the signs of anxiety and seeking appropriate support and treatment, individuals can learn to cope with stress and anxiety in a healthy way. Therapy, medication, lifestyle changes, and self-care practices all play a role in managing anxiety symptoms and improving overall quality of life. It is important to remember that anxiety is a common and treatable condition, and with the right support and resources, individuals can learn to navigate their anxiety symptoms and live a fulfilling and meaningful life.

- Calming the mind with mindfulness

Mindfulness has gained significant popularity in recent years as a powerful tool for calming the mind and reducing stress. It is a practice that involves paying attention to the present moment without judgment. By focusing on the present moment, individuals can become more aware of their thoughts and feelings and learn to manage them more effectively. This can lead to a sense of calm and relaxation that can help to improve mental well-being.

One of the key principles of mindfulness is acceptance. This involves acknowledging and accepting your thoughts and feelings without judging them or trying to change them. By accepting your thoughts and feelings, you can learn to let go of negative emotions and find inner peace. This can be particularly helpful for individuals who struggle with anxiety or depression, as it can help to break the cycle of negative thinking and bring a sense of calmness and clarity.

Mindfulness can also help individuals to develop a greater sense of self-awareness. By paying attention to the present moment, individuals can become more aware of their thoughts, emotions, and physical sensations. This can help them to better understand themselves and their reactions to different situations. By increasing self-awareness, individuals can also learn to recognize and manage their emotions more effectively, leading to a greater sense of control and well-being.

Furthermore, mindfulness can help individuals to improve their focus and concentration. In today's fast-paced world, many of us are constantly bombarded with distractions that can make it difficult to stay focused on the task at hand. By practicing mindfulness, individuals can learn to stay present and focused, even in the face of distractions. This can help to improve productivity and efficiency in both personal and professional life.

Another key benefit of mindfulness is its ability to improve relationships. By becoming more present and attentive in interactions with others, individuals can develop a deeper connection and understanding with those around them. This can lead to improved communication, empathy, and compassion, which are essential for building strong and healthy relationships. By cultivating these qualities through mindfulness, individuals can create more meaningful and fulfilling connections with others. By practicing mindfulness, individuals can learn to accept and manage their thoughts and feelings, develop greater self-awareness, improve focus and concentration, and enhance relationships with others. By incorporating mindfulness into daily life, individuals can experience a profound sense of calm and well-being that can help them to navigate the challenges of life with greater ease and resilience.

- Building resiliency against anxiety

Anxiety is a common mental health issue that affects millions of people worldwide. It can manifest in various forms, from generalized anxiety disorder to panic attacks to social anxiety. While some level of anxiety is normal and even helpful in certain situations, excessive and persistent anxiety can be debilitating and impact one's quality of life. Building resiliency against anxiety involves developing coping strategies and skills to navigate stressful situations and manage anxiety triggers effectively.

One key component of building resiliency against anxiety is understanding the root causes of anxiety. Anxiety can be triggered by a variety of factors, including genetic predisposition, environmental stressors, traumatic experiences, and underlying health conditions. By identifying the underlying causes of anxiety, individuals can better address and manage their symptoms. Additionally, understanding the role of neurotransmitters such as serotonin and dopamine in anxiety can help individuals make informed decisions about their treatment options.

Another important aspect of building resiliency against anxiety is developing healthy coping mechanisms. This includes practicing self-care techniques, such as exercise, meditation, and mindfulness, to reduce stress and promote emotional well-being. Engaging in activities that bring joy and relaxation, such as spending time in nature, pursuing hobbies, and connecting with loved ones, can also help alleviate anxiety symptoms. Additionally, seeking support from a therapist or counselor can provide individuals with the tools and resources they need to effectively manage their anxiety.

In addition to developing healthy coping mechanisms, building resiliency against anxiety involves creating a supportive environment that fosters emotional well-being. This includes surrounding oneself with positive and uplifting people who provide encouragement and validation. Building strong social connections and maintaining healthy relationships can help individuals feel supported and less isolated in their struggles with anxiety. Additionally, creating a safe and nurturing physical environment, such as a clutter-free home or workspace, can help reduce feelings of overwhelm and anxiety.

Building resiliency against anxiety also requires developing effective communication skills to express one's thoughts and feelings in a healthy and constructive manner. Learning how to set boundaries, assert oneself, and communicate effectively with others can help reduce feelings of stress and anxiety. Additionally, practicing active listening and empathy can enhance interpersonal relationships and reduce conflict, which can contribute to feelings of anxiety. By improving communication skills, individuals can better navigate challenging situations and manage their anxiety effectively.

Moreover, building resiliency against anxiety involves cultivating a positive mindset and reframing negative thought patterns. Cognitive-behavioral therapy (CBT) is a widely used therapeutic approach that helps individuals identify and challenge distorted thinking patterns that contribute to anxiety. By replacing negative thoughts with more balanced and realistic ones, individuals can gain a sense of control over their anxiety and improve their overall well-being. Additionally, practicing gratitude and focusing on positive aspects of life can help shift one's perspective and mindset, leading to greater emotional resilience. By incorporating these strategies into one's daily routine and seeking support from professionals when needed, individuals can effectively manage their anxiety and improve their overall well-being. With dedication, perseverance, and the right tools, it is possible to build resiliency against anxiety and lead a more fulfilling and balanced life.

Chapter 14: Cultivating Patience and Resilience

- DEVELOPING PATIENCE through mindfulness

Developing patience through mindfulness is a powerful practice that can bring about a transformation in how we approach challenges, interact with others, and navigate the ups and downs of daily life. Patience is not just about waiting for things to happen or tolerating difficult situations, but it is also about cultivating a sense of calm, resilience, and presence in the moment. Mindfulness is a practice that involves paying attention to the present moment without judgment, and it can help us develop the ability to be patient by teaching us to respond to challenges with greater awareness and equanimity.

One of the key ways that mindfulness helps us develop patience is by bringing our attention to the present moment. Often, impatience arises when we are caught up in thoughts about the past or worrying about the future. When we are focused on the present moment, we are better able to see things as they are, rather than getting caught up in our own expectations or desires. This allows us to respond to situations with greater clarity and objectivity, rather than reacting impulsively out of frustration or anger. By practicing mindfulness, we can learn to observe our thoughts and feelings without getting entangled in them, which can help us cultivate a sense of patience and perspective in the face of challenges.

Mindfulness also helps us develop patience by teaching us to cultivate a sense of acceptance and non-judgment towards ourselves and others. When we practice mindfulness, we learn to approach our experiences with an attitude of curiosity and openness, rather than trying to control or judge them. This can help us develop a more compassionate and understanding attitude towards ourselves and others, which can be a key component of developing patience. By accepting things as they are, rather than constantly trying to change or fix them, we can approach challenges with a greater sense of calm and ease, which can help us navigate difficult situations with greater patience and grace.

Another way that mindfulness helps us develop patience is by helping us cultivate a sense of equanimity in the face of difficult emotions or situations. By practicing mindfulness, we can learn to observe our emotions without getting swept away by them, which can help us develop a greater sense of emotional resilience and stability. This can be particularly helpful in cultivating patience, as it can help us respond to challenges with a greater sense of calm and balance, rather than reacting impulsively out of fear or frustration. By learning to sit with our emotions without getting caught up in them, we can develop the strength and ability to navigate difficult situations with greater patience and grace. By bringing our attention to the present moment, cultivating acceptance and non-judgment, and building emotional resilience, we can develop the ability to respond to challenges with patience and grace. Mindfulness offers us a way to cultivate a deeper sense of presence and awareness in the moment, which can help us develop the ability to approach difficulties with a greater sense of calm and balance. Ultimately, cultivating patience through mindfulness can help us live more fully and authentically, with a greater sense of peace and well-being in our lives.

- Embracing challenges with resilience

Resilience is a trait that is essential for navigating the ups and downs of life, particularly when faced with challenges. It is the ability to bounce back from setbacks, adapt to change, and thrive in the face of adversity. Embracing challenges with resilience means approaching difficulties with a positive attitude, a willingness to learn and grow, and a determination to overcome obstacles. It is about staying calm, focused, and optimistic in the face of adversity, and finding the strength and courage to keep moving forward.

One of the key aspects of embracing challenges with resilience is having a growth mindset. This means believing that challenges are an opportunity for growth and development, rather than a roadblock to success. When faced with a difficult situation, resilient individuals see it as a chance to learn, to develop new skills, and to improve themselves. They embrace challenges with a sense of curiosity and optimism, knowing that they have the ability to overcome obstacles and come out stronger on the other side.

In order to embrace challenges with resilience, it is important to cultivate a sense of self-awareness. This means being in tune with your thoughts, emotions, and reactions to difficult situations. By understanding your own strengths and weaknesses, as well as your triggers and coping mechanisms, you can better navigate challenges and setbacks. Self-awareness allows you to identify potential obstacles, develop strategies for overcoming them, and build a support system to help you stay on track.

Another important aspect of embracing challenges with resilience is developing effective coping strategies. This may include practicing self-care, such as getting enough rest, exercise, and healthy nutrition, as well as engaging in activities that bring you joy and relaxation. It may also involve seeking support from friends, family, or a therapist, and learning healthy ways to manage stress and anxiety. By developing a toolkit of coping strategies, you can better navigate challenges and setbacks, and build the resilience needed to overcome obstacles.

In addition to self-awareness and effective coping strategies, it is also important to cultivate a strong sense of purpose and meaning in life. This can help you stay motivated and focused when faced with difficulties, and provide a sense of direction and inspiration to keep moving forward. By connecting with your values, passions, and goals, you can find the inner strength and resilience needed to face challenges head-on, and work towards achieving your dreams and aspirations.

Ultimately, embracing challenges with resilience is about facing adversity with courage, determination, and a positive mindset. It is about believing in your own abilities, learning from setbacks, and staying committed to your goals and values. By cultivating self-awareness, effective coping strategies, and a sense of purpose and meaning, you can build the resilience needed to navigate life's challenges and come out stronger on the other side. With resilience as your compass, you can embrace challenges as opportunities for growth and transformation, and ultimately thrive in the face of adversity.

- Building inner strength through mindfulness practices

In today's fast-paced world, many people find themselves struggling to cope with the demands and pressures of everyday life. Whether it's work, relationships, or personal challenges, it's easy to feel overwhelmed and out of control. However, there is a powerful tool that can help us navigate these challenges with grace and resilience: mindfulness practices. By cultivating mindfulness, we can build inner strength and resilience that can help us face difficult situations with calmness and clarity.

Mindfulness is the practice of bringing our attention to the present moment, without judgment or attachment. It involves paying attention to our thoughts, feelings, and sensations in a gentle and compassionate way. Through regular mindfulness practice, we can learn to cultivate a sense of inner peace and well-being that can help us deal with stress and adversity.

One of the key ways that mindfulness can help us build inner strength is by increasing our self-awareness. When we practice mindfulness, we become more attuned to our thoughts, emotions, and physical sensations. This increased awareness can help us recognize when we are feeling overwhelmed or stressed, and can allow us to take steps to address these feelings before they escalate. By learning to tune into our inner experiences, we can develop a deeper understanding of ourselves and cultivate a sense of inner strength that can help us navigate life's challenges with resilience and grace.

Mindfulness can also help us develop greater emotional regulation skills. When we are mindful, we are better able to observe our emotions without getting caught up in them. This can help us avoid reacting impulsively or inappropriately when faced with difficult situations. By practicing mindfulness, we can learn to respond to stressful or triggering events with a sense of calm and poise, rather than succumbing to reactive behavior. This can help us build inner strength and resilience, as we learn to navigate difficult emotions with grace and compassion.

In addition to helping us build inner strength, mindfulness practices can also improve our overall well-being. Research has shown that regular mindfulness practice can reduce stress, anxiety, and depression, and can improve overall emotional and physical health. By cultivating mindfulness, we can learn to approach life with a sense of ease and acceptance, rather than getting caught up in worry or rumination. This can help us build resilience in the face of life's challenges, and can empower us to live more fully and authentically.

There are many different ways to cultivate mindfulness in our lives. One of the most common practices is mindfulness meditation, where we sit quietly and observe our thoughts and sensations without judgment. Mindfulness can also be practiced informally throughout the day, by taking moments to pause and tune into our present-moment experience. Whether we choose to incorporate mindfulness into our daily routine through formal meditation practice or through informal mindfulness activities, the key is to cultivate a sense of presence and awareness in our lives. By cultivating mindfulness, we can develop self-awareness, emotional regulation skills, and overall well-being that can help us face difficult situations with calmness and clarity. Whether we choose to incorporate formal mindfulness meditation practice or informal mindfulness activities into our daily routine, the key is to cultivate a sense of presence and awareness that can help us build resilience and inner strength in the face of life's challenges. Mindfulness is a powerful tool that can empower us to live more fully and authentically, and to approach life with a sense of ease and acceptance.

Chapter 15: Mindfulness in Daily Life

- INTEGRATING MINDFULNESS into daily routines

In recent years, there has been a growing interest in the practice of mindfulness and its potential benefits for mental well-being. Mindfulness, as defined by Jon Kabat-Zinn, is the awareness that arises through paying attention, on purpose, in the present moment, non-judgmentally. Essentially, mindfulness involves being fully present and engaged with whatever is happening in the moment, without being distracted by thoughts about the past or worries about the future. While mindfulness has its roots in ancient contemplative practices, it has gained popularity in modern Western psychology as a tool for reducing stress, improving focus, and enhancing overall quality of life.

One of the key challenges facing individuals interested in integrating mindfulness into their daily routines is finding the time and motivation to practice consistently. Many people lead busy lives filled with obligations and commitments, making it difficult to carve out dedicated time for mindfulness practice. However, the beauty of mindfulness is that it can be incorporated into everyday activities, such as eating, walking, or even washing dishes. By bringing attention to the present moment and cultivating an attitude of non-judgmental awareness, individuals can infuse mindfulness into their daily routines without adding extra time or effort.

One simple way to integrate mindfulness into daily routines is to practice mindful breathing. This involves taking a few moments throughout the day to focus on the sensation of the breath entering and leaving the body. By tuning into the rhythm of the breath and observing it without trying to change it, individuals can anchor themselves in the present moment and cultivate a sense of calm and centeredness. Mindful breathing can be practiced while waiting in line, sitting in traffic, or even during a work meeting. By incorporating this simple practice into daily activities, individuals can begin to strengthen their mindfulness muscles and build a foundation for more formal meditation practice.

Another effective way to integrate mindfulness into daily routines is to engage in mindful movement practices, such as yoga or tai chi. These forms of exercise not only promote physical health and flexibility but also encourage mindfulness by emphasizing the connection between body and mind. By focusing on the sensations of movement and breath during yoga or tai chi practice, individuals can cultivate a sense of embodied awareness and presence. These practices offer a unique opportunity to combine physical exercise with mindfulness, making them ideal for individuals looking to infuse mindfulness into their daily routines in a holistic way.

In addition to mindfulness practices like mindful breathing and mindful movement, individuals can also incorporate mindfulness into everyday activities such as eating, drinking, and even working. Mindful eating, for example, involves paying attention to the taste, texture, and smell of food while eating, as well as noticing hunger and fullness cues. By savoring each bite and eating without distractions, individuals can cultivate a greater appreciation for food and a more mindful relationship with eating. Similarly, mindful drinking involves savoring each sip of a beverage, whether it be a cup of tea or a glass of water, and being fully present to the experience of drinking. By bringing mindfulness to these everyday activities, individuals can enhance their overall sense of well-being and satisfaction.

In the workplace, mindfulness can be a powerful tool for reducing stress and enhancing focus and productivity. By incorporating short mindfulness practices into the workday, such as a brief breathing exercise or a moment of mindful walking, individuals can create space for self-care and mental clarity amidst the demands of a busy job. Mindfulness can also be applied to tasks such as email management, meeting facilitation, and decision-making, by bringing a sense of present-moment awareness and non-reactivity to these activities. By cultivating mindfulness in the workplace, individuals can not only improve their own well-being but also contribute to a more positive and productive work environment for their colleagues. By incorporating mindfulness practices such as mindful breathing, mindful movement, and mindful eating into everyday activities, individuals can cultivate a greater sense of presence, awareness, and appreciation for the present moment. Whether at home, at work, or in leisure activities, mindfulness offers a practical and accessible way to infuse daily life with a sense of calm, clarity, and connection. By making a commitment to practice mindfulness regularly and with intention, individuals can tap into the transformative power of mindfulness and reap the benefits of a more mindful and fulfilling life.

- Finding moments of mindfulness throughout the day

In today's fast-paced world, finding moments of mindfulness throughout the day can seem like a challenging task. With the constant barrage of notifications, deadlines, and obligations, it can be easy to get caught up in the hustle and bustle of daily life and forget to take a moment to pause and breathe. However, incorporating mindfulness into your daily routine can have a profound impact on your overall well-being and mental health.

Mindfulness is a practice that involves paying attention to the present moment with a non-judgmental and accepting attitude. It involves tuning into your thoughts, feelings, and sensations in a calm and focused way. By cultivating mindfulness throughout the day, you can increase your awareness of your thoughts and emotions, reduce stress and anxiety, and improve your overall sense of well-being.

One way to find moments of mindfulness throughout the day is to incorporate short mindfulness practices into your routine. This can be as simple as taking a few minutes to focus on your breath, observe the sensations in your body, or tune into your surroundings. You can set reminders on your phone or use mindfulness apps to help you remember to take these short breaks throughout the day. By incorporating these mini mindfulness practices into your routine, you can cultivate a sense of calm and presence in your day.

Another way to find moments of mindfulness throughout the day is to engage in everyday activities with mindful awareness. This can include tasks such as eating, walking, or even washing the dishes. By bringing your full attention to these activities and noticing the sensations, thoughts, and feelings that arise, you can turn these mundane tasks into opportunities for mindfulness. By focusing on the present moment and letting go of distracting thoughts and worries, you can cultivate a sense of peace and relaxation in your day.

Additionally, taking time to connect with nature can be a powerful way to find moments of mindfulness throughout the day. Whether it's taking a walk in the park, sitting outside in your backyard, or simply gazing out the window at the sky, spending time in nature can help you feel more grounded and connected to the present moment. The sights, sounds, and smells of the natural world can serve as a powerful anchor for your attention and help you let go of stress and distractions.

Incorporating mindfulness into your daily routine can also involve setting aside dedicated time for formal mindfulness practices, such as meditation or yoga. carving out time for these practices can help you deepen your mindfulness skills and cultivate a sense of inner peace and stillness. Even just a few minutes of meditation or gentle yoga can help you relax and reset your mind, allowing you to approach the rest of your day with a sense of calm and clarity.

It's important to remember that mindfulness is not about achieving a state of perfect calm or eliminating all of your thoughts and emotions. Rather, it's about cultivating a sense of awareness and acceptance of whatever is happening in the present moment. By finding moments of mindfulness throughout the day, you can increase your capacity to stay present, focused, and grounded in the midst of life's challenges and distractions. By incorporating short mindfulness practices into your routine, engaging in everyday activities with mindful awareness, connecting with nature, and setting aside time for formal mindfulness practices, you can cultivate a sense of calm, presence, and inner peace in your day. Remember that mindfulness is a skill that takes practice and patience, so be gentle with yourself as you embark on this journey. By making mindfulness a priority in your daily life, you can experience a greater sense of clarity, balance, and resilience in the face of life's ups and downs.

- Enhancing overall life satisfaction through mindfulness

This ancient practice, rooted in Eastern philosophies such as Buddhism, involves being fully present and engaged in the moment, without judgment or attachment to the past or future. By cultivating mindfulness, individuals can develop a greater sense of self-awareness and emotional regulation, leading to improved mental health and well-being. In our fast-paced, technology-driven world, it is all too easy to become overwhelmed by the demands of work, family, and social obligations. This constant state of busyness can take a toll on our mental and physical health, leading to feelings of stress and anxiety. However, by practicing mindfulness, individuals can learn to quiet the mind and focus on the present moment, allowing them to let go of worry and rumination. This can help to reduce levels of cortisol, the stress hormone, and promote a sense of calm and relaxation. When we are able to observe our thoughts and emotions without reacting impulsively, we are better able to choose how we respond to challenging situations. This can help us to break free from negative patterns of thinking and behavior, leading to more positive outcomes in our relationships, work, and daily lives. By developing a greater sense of emotional intelligence through mindfulness, individuals can cultivate healthier and more fulfilling interactions with others, resulting in a greater sense of life satisfaction. Through the practice of mindfulness, individuals are encouraged to turn inward and explore their thoughts, feelings, and beliefs without judgment. This can help us to become more aware of our innermost desires and values, enabling us to make decisions that are aligned with our authentic selves. By cultivating self-awareness, individuals can also develop a greater sense of self-compassion and acceptance, allowing them to embrace their strengths and weaknesses with kindness and understanding. This can lead to a greater sense of fulfillment and purpose in life, as individuals are able to live in alignment with their true selves. In our fast-paced society, it is all too easy to get caught up in the pursuit of material wealth and success, leading us to overlook the simple joys and blessings that surround us each day. By practicing mindfulness, individuals can learn to slow down and pay attention to the beauty and wonder of the world around them, fostering a greater sense of gratitude and awe. This can help us to cultivate a more positive outlook on life, leading to increased feelings of happiness and contentment. By reducing stress and anxiety, improving emotional regulation, increasing self-awareness and acceptance, and promoting gratitude and appreciation, mindfulness empowers individuals to live more fulfilling and meaningful lives. As we continue to navigate the challenges of modern life, incorporating mindfulness into our daily routine can help us to cultivate a greater sense of well-being and satisfaction, enabling us to thrive in all areas of our lives.

Chapter 16: Self-Compassion Meditation

- PRACTICING KINDNESS and compassion towards oneself

Practicing kindness and compassion towards oneself is an essential aspect of overall well-being and mental health. In today's fast-paced and high-pressure world, it can be easy to neglect self-care and prioritize the needs of others over our own. However, taking the time to nurture and care for ourselves is not selfish, but rather necessary for personal growth and happiness.

One of the first steps in practicing kindness and compassion towards oneself is acknowledging and accepting our own humanity. We are all imperfect beings and will inevitably make mistakes and face challenges in our lives. It is important to be gentle with ourselves in these moments and not be too harsh or critical. Instead of dwelling on past mistakes or perceived failures, it is essential to practice self-forgiveness and move forward with a sense of self-compassion.

Self-compassion involves treating ourselves with the same kindness and understanding that we would offer to a close friend or loved one. This means being mindful of our thoughts and emotions and responding to ourselves with empathy and care. When we practice self-compassion, we are better able to cope with difficult situations, manage stress, and maintain a positive mindset.

In addition to self-compassion, it is important to cultivate self-kindness in our daily lives. This involves engaging in behaviors and activities that support our physical, emotional, and spiritual well-being. This could include setting aside time for self-care activities such as exercise, meditation, or relaxation techniques. It also involves practicing self-love and gratitude for the unique qualities and strengths that we possess.

Another important aspect of practicing kindness and compassion towards oneself is setting boundaries and prioritizing our own needs. It can be easy to fall into the trap of people-pleasing and sacrificing our own well-being for the sake of others. However, it is essential to establish healthy boundaries and learn to say no when necessary. By prioritizing our own needs and desires, we demonstrate self-respect and strengthen our sense of self-worth.

In times of difficulty or adversity, practicing kindness and compassion towards oneself can be a powerful tool for resilience and self-healing. When faced with challenges, it is important to acknowledge our feelings and emotions without judgment and offer ourselves comfort and support. This could involve seeking out the help of a trusted friend, therapist, or mentor, as well as engaging in self-care practices that promote relaxation and emotional well-being.

Ultimately, practicing kindness and compassion towards oneself is an ongoing process that requires patience, self-awareness, and dedication. By cultivating self-love and self-compassion, we can enhance our overall well-being, build resilience in the face of adversity, and lead a more fulfilling and balanced life. So, let us commit to treating ourselves with kindness and compassion, embracing our imperfections, and nurturing our inner selves with love and care. We deserve it.

- Overcoming self-criticism and doubt

Self-criticism and doubt are common experiences that many people face at some point in their lives. These feelings can be overwhelming and can hinder personal growth and success if not addressed properly. It is important to acknowledge and understand these feelings in order to overcome them and move forward confidently.

Self-criticism often stems from a lack of self-confidence and a fear of failure. It can be the result of negative self-talk and internalized beliefs about one's abilities and worth. It is important to challenge and reframe these negative thoughts in order to build a more positive self-image. By practicing self-compassion and cultivating self-awareness, individuals can begin to recognize their strengths and accomplishments, rather than focusing solely on their perceived flaws and shortcomings.

Doubt, on the other hand, is often fueled by fear and insecurity. It can manifest as a lack of faith in one's abilities or a fear of making mistakes. It is important to acknowledge that doubt is a normal part of the human experience and that everyone experiences it at some point. By reframing doubt as an opportunity for growth and learning, individuals can begin to see it as a stepping stone towards success rather than a roadblock.

One strategy for overcoming self-criticism and doubt is to practice self-compassion and self-care. This involves treating oneself with kindness and understanding, rather than harsh judgment. By engaging in activities that bring joy and fulfillment, individuals can boost their self-esteem and confidence. This can help counteract negative self-talk and build a more positive mindset.

Another important strategy is to challenge negative thoughts and beliefs through cognitive restructuring. This involves identifying and disputing irrational or unhelpful beliefs that contribute to self-criticism and doubt. By recognizing these patterns and replacing them with more realistic and positive thoughts, individuals can begin to shift their mindset and build a more resilient sense of self.

Additionally, seeking support from friends, family, or a therapist can be helpful in overcoming self-criticism and doubt. Talking about one's feelings and experiences with others can provide validation and perspective, and can help individuals gain clarity and insight into their struggles. This can also help individuals feel less isolated and more connected to others, which can be a powerful antidote to self-doubt. By practicing self-compassion, challenging negative thoughts, and seeking support, individuals can begin to overcome these barriers and build a more resilient and confident sense of self. It is important to remember that change takes time and effort, and that progress may not always be linear. However, by committing to self-care and self-growth, individuals can begin to cultivate a more positive and fulfilling life.

- Building self-worth through self-compassion

Building self-worth through self-compassion is an essential aspect of personal growth and development. Self-worth refers to the belief in one's own inherent value and worth as a human being. It is closely related to self-esteem, which is an individual's overall evaluation of their own worth and capabilities. Self-compassion, on the other hand, involves treating oneself with kindness, understanding, and acceptance in the face of imperfections and struggles. By cultivating self-compassion, individuals can enhance their self-worth and develop a more positive self-concept.

One of the key components of building self-worth through self-compassion is practicing self-acceptance. This involves acknowledging and embracing both the positive and negative aspects of oneself without judgment or criticism. Self-acceptance is about recognizing that no one is perfect and that it is okay to have flaws and imperfections. By accepting oneself as a whole, individuals can develop a more realistic and compassionate view of themselves, which can enhance their self-worth.

Another important aspect of building self-worth through self-compassion is practicing self-kindness. This involves treating oneself with the same care, warmth, and understanding that one would offer to a close friend in times of need. Self-kindness allows individuals to be gentle and nurturing towards themselves, especially when facing challenges or setbacks. By cultivating a mindset of self-compassion and kindness, individuals can develop a greater sense of self-worth and self-esteem.

In addition to self-acceptance and self-kindness, developing self-compassion also involves cultivating mindfulness. Mindfulness is the practice of being fully present and aware of one's thoughts, feelings, and sensations without judgment or attachment. By practicing mindfulness, individuals can become more attuned to their inner experiences and develop a greater sense of self-awareness. This can help individuals to identify and challenge negative self-talk and beliefs that may be undermining their self-worth.

Building self-worth through self-compassion also involves practicing self-forgiveness. Self-forgiveness is the act of letting go of self-blame, guilt, and regret for past mistakes or shortcomings. It is about acknowledging one's humanness and recognizing that everyone makes mistakes. By practicing self-forgiveness, individuals can release themselves from the burden of self-criticism and develop a greater sense of self-compassion and self-worth.

It is important to note that building self-worth through self-compassion is a gradual and ongoing process that requires patience and commitment. It may involve challenging deeply ingrained beliefs and patterns of self-criticism that have been developed over time. However, with practice and persistence, individuals can cultivate a more positive and compassionate relationship with themselves, which can lead to greater self-worth and overall well-being. By cultivating self-acceptance, self-kindness, mindfulness, and self-forgiveness, individuals can develop a more compassionate and nurturing relationship with themselves. This can lead to greater self-confidence, resilience, and overall well-being. Ultimately, by building self-worth through self-compassion, individuals can foster a deeper sense of self-acceptance and self-love, which are essential for personal growth and fulfillment.

Chapter 17: Stress Reduction Techniques

- MINDFULNESS-BASED stress reduction strategies

Mindfulness-based stress reduction (MBSR) strategies have gained popularity in recent years as a way to combat the negative effects of stress on both our physical and mental well-being. Developed by Jon Kabat-Zinn in the 1970s, MBSR is a structured program that combines mindfulness meditation, body awareness, and yoga to help individuals cope with stress, anxiety, and other emotional challenges. The core components of MBSR include mindfulness meditation practices, body scan exercises, gentle yoga movements, and group discussions to explore the connection between thoughts, emotions, and physical sensations.

One of the key principles of MBSR is the concept of mindfulness, which involves paying attention to the present moment without judgment. This can help individuals become more aware of their thoughts and feelings, and develop a greater sense of self-awareness and self-compassion. By practicing mindfulness, individuals can learn to recognize when they are experiencing stress and develop strategies to manage it in a healthy way. This can lead to a reduction in stress-related symptoms such as anxiety, depression, and chronic pain.

Another important aspect of MBSR is the body scan exercise, which involves systematically focusing on different parts of the body and bringing awareness to physical sensations, tension, and discomfort. This practice can help individuals identify areas of tension and release physical stress, leading to a greater sense of relaxation and well-being. Through regular practice, individuals can become more attuned to their body and develop a greater sense of embodiment, which can help them better manage stressful situations.

In addition to mindfulness meditation and body scan exercises, MBSR also incorporates gentle yoga movements to help individuals cultivate a mind-body connection and reduce physical tension. Yoga can help individuals release physical stress and improve flexibility, strength, and balance. By combining mindfulness meditation, body scan exercises, and yoga, individuals can develop a holistic approach to stress reduction that addresses both the mind and body.

Group discussions are also an important component of MBSR, as they provide individuals with the opportunity to share their experiences, insights, and challenges with others in a supportive and non-judgmental environment. By connecting with others who are also on the mindfulness journey, individuals can feel a sense of community and camaraderie, which can provide additional support and motivation to continue practicing mindfulness. Group discussions can also help individuals gain new perspectives and insights on how to apply mindfulness in their daily lives. By integrating mindfulness meditation, body scan exercises, yoga, and group discussions, individuals can develop a comprehensive toolkit for managing stress and building resilience.

- Coping with stress in healthy ways

Stress is an inevitable part of life, and how we cope with it can have a significant impact on our overall well-being. While some stress is normal and even helpful in certain situations, chronic stress can have detrimental effects on both our physical and mental health. It is essential to have effective coping mechanisms in place to manage stress in healthy ways.

One of the most important aspects of coping with stress is recognizing when it is becoming overwhelming. This involves being mindful of your emotions and physical sensations and understanding how they may be connected to stress. Signs of chronic stress can include irritability, fatigue, headaches, muscle tension, and difficulty concentrating. By paying attention to these warning signs, you can take proactive steps to address stress before it escalates.

Once you have identified that you are experiencing stress, it is important to find healthy ways to cope. One of the most effective strategies is to engage in regular physical activity. Exercise has been shown to release endorphins, which are natural mood lifters that can help reduce stress and anxiety. Whether it's going for a run, taking a yoga class, or simply going for a walk outside, finding a form of exercise that you enjoy can be a powerful tool in managing stress.

In addition to exercise, practicing relaxation techniques can also be beneficial in coping with stress. Techniques such as deep breathing, meditation, and progressive muscle relaxation can help calm the mind and body, reducing feelings of stress and tension. These practices can be particularly helpful when done regularly, as they can help to lower overall levels of stress and increase your resilience to future stressors.

Another important aspect of coping with stress is maintaining a healthy lifestyle. This includes eating a balanced diet, getting enough sleep, and avoiding unhealthy coping mechanisms such as excessive alcohol consumption or drug use. When we take care of our physical health, we are better equipped to handle the challenges that come our way. Additionally, seeking support from friends, family, or a therapist can also be beneficial in coping with stress. Talking about your feelings and receiving validation and support from others can help alleviate feelings of isolation and provide a sense of comfort and understanding. By being mindful of our emotions and physical sensations, engaging in regular physical activity, practicing relaxation techniques, maintaining a healthy lifestyle, and seeking support from others, we can effectively manage stress and reduce its negative effects on our health. Remember that it is okay to ask for help when needed, and that taking care of yourself is essential in coping with stress in a healthy manner.

- Creating a stress-free mindset

Creating a stress-free mindset is essential for maintaining overall well-being and productivity in both personal and professional life. Stress is a natural response that our bodies have to challenging situations, but when it becomes chronic or overwhelming, it can have serious effects on our physical and mental health. By cultivating a stress-free mindset, we can learn to manage stress more effectively and improve our quality of life.

One of the first steps in creating a stress-free mindset is to identify the sources of stress in your life. This may be related to work, relationships, financial concerns, health issues, or any number of factors. By pinpointing the specific triggers of your stress, you can begin to address them more effectively. This might involve making changes in your daily routine, setting boundaries with people who cause you stress, seeking support from friends or a therapist, or developing coping strategies to better manage stressful situations.

Another important aspect of cultivating a stress-free mindset is to practice self-care and prioritize your own well-being. This means taking time for yourself to relax, recharge, and engage in activities that bring you joy and fulfillment. Whether it's spending time in nature, practicing yoga or meditation, reading a book, or pursuing a hobby, self-care is essential for reducing stress and promoting overall wellness. By making self-care a priority in your daily routine, you can build resilience and better cope with the challenges that come your way.

In addition to self-care, developing a positive mindset can also help in reducing stress and promoting a sense of well-being. By reframing negative thoughts and focusing on gratitude, optimism, and self-compassion, you can shift your perspective and approach to stressful situations. This might involve practicing mindfulness, affirmations, or cognitive-behavioral techniques to cultivate a more positive outlook on life. By fostering a sense of gratitude for the good things in your life and learning to be kinder to yourself, you can build resilience and better cope with stress.

Furthermore, maintaining a healthy lifestyle, including regular exercise, a balanced diet, and adequate sleep, is crucial for managing stress and promoting overall well-being. Physical activity releases endorphins, the body's natural stress relievers, and helps to reduce anxiety and improve mood. Eating a nutritious diet that is high in fruits, vegetables, whole grains, and lean proteins can also help to support your body's stress response and overall health. Additionally, getting enough restful sleep is essential for recharging your body and mind, reducing stress, and improving cognitive function. By identifying the sources of stress in your life, practicing self-care, developing a positive mindset, and maintaining a healthy lifestyle, you can better manage stress and promote overall well-being. With dedication and mindfulness, you can cultivate a sense of calm, resilience, and inner peace that will serve you well in navigating life's challenges and uncertainties. Remember to be patient and kind to yourself as you work towards creating a stress-free mindset, and seek support from friends, family, or a mental health professional when needed. By prioritizing your well-being and taking proactive steps to manage stress, you can build a foundation for a more balanced and joyful life.

Chapter 18: Mindful Parenting

- USING MINDFULNESS to be present with children

Mindfulness is a powerful tool that can be used to cultivate presence and awareness in our daily interactions with children. By practicing mindfulness, we can learn to be fully present with children, to listen to them with open hearts and minds, and to respond to their needs in a compassionate and empathetic way. By being more present with children, we can deepen our connections with them, build trust and rapport, and create a safe and nurturing environment in which they can thrive and grow.

One of the key components of mindfulness is being fully present in the moment, without judgment or distraction. When we are fully present with children, we are able to tune into their needs and emotions with clarity and focus. We can listen to them with full attention, without being consumed by our own thoughts, worries, or distractions. This level of presence allows us to truly connect with children on a deeper level, to understand their perspectives, and to respond to them in a way that is compassionate and supportive.

In addition to being present with children, mindfulness can also help us regulate our own emotions and reactions, which in turn can have a positive impact on our interactions with children. When we practice mindfulness, we become more aware of our own thoughts, emotions, and triggers, and we learn to respond to them with greater awareness and self-compassion. This self-awareness allows us to respond to children from a place of calm and centeredness, rather than reacting impulsively or emotionally. By regulating our own emotions in this way, we can create a more peaceful and harmonious environment for children, in which they feel safe and supported.

Furthermore, mindfulness can help us cultivate empathy and compassion towards children, which is essential for building strong and positive relationships with them. By practicing mindfulness, we can develop greater empathy by tuning into the emotions and needs of children, and responding to them with care and understanding. This kind of empathetic listening can help children feel seen, heard, and valued, which in turn can strengthen their sense of self-worth and enhance their emotional well-being. By approaching children with compassion and empathy, we can create a nurturing and supportive environment in which they can thrive and reach their full potential.

Incorporating mindfulness into our interactions with children can also help us to become more attuned to their individual needs and preferences. By being fully present with children, we can notice subtle cues and signals that indicate their emotional state, their interests, and their preferences. This level of awareness allows us to tailor our interactions with children to meet their specific needs and preferences, which in turn can help them feel understood and supported. By practicing mindfulness in this way, we can create a more responsive and personalized approach to interacting with children, which can enhance their sense of autonomy and agency in their own lives. By being fully present with children, we can listen to them with open hearts and minds, respond to their needs with compassion and empathy, and create a safe and nurturing environment in which they can thrive and grow. By practicing mindfulness in our interactions with children, we can regulate our own emotions and reactions, cultivate empathy and compassion, and become more attuned to their individual needs and preferences. Ultimately, mindfulness can help us to build strong and positive relationships with children, and to create a supportive and nurturing environment in which they can flourish and reach their full potential.

- Managing stress and emotions as a parent

Parenting is a rewarding yet challenging experience that can often lead to feelings of stress and overwhelm. As parents, we are responsible for the well-being and upbringing of our children, which can feel like a heavy burden at times. However, it is important for us to recognize that managing stress and emotions is crucial for our own mental health and for the health of our families.

By learning how to effectively cope with stress and regulate our emotions, we can create a more harmonious and peaceful environment in our homes.

One of the first steps in managing stress and emotions as a parent is to recognize the signs and symptoms of stress. Stress can manifest in a variety of ways, including physical symptoms such as headaches, muscle tension, and fatigue, as well as emotional symptoms such as irritability, anxiety, and depression. By paying attention to these signs, we can become more aware of when we are feeling stressed and take steps to address it before it escalates. It can also be helpful to identify triggers that may be contributing to our stress, such as financial concerns, relationship issues, or work pressures.

Once we have identified our stressors, it is essential to develop healthy coping mechanisms to manage them effectively. This could include engaging in regular exercise, practicing relaxation techniques such as deep breathing or meditation, or seeking support from friends, family, or a therapist. It is important to find activities that help to reduce stress and promote feelings of relaxation and well-being, as this can have a significant impact on our overall mental health and emotional resilience.

In addition to managing stress, it is crucial for parents to learn how to regulate their emotions in a healthy way. This means being aware of our emotions, understanding what triggers them, and learning how to express them in a constructive manner. Emotions such as anger, frustration, and sadness are normal and natural responses to the challenges of parenting, but it is important to express these emotions in a way that is respectful and non-destructive.

One effective strategy for regulating emotions as a parent is practicing mindfulness. Mindfulness is the practice of being present in the moment, without judgment or attachment to thoughts or feelings. By cultivating a mindfulness practice, we can become more aware of our emotions as they arise and learn to respond to them in a calm and rational manner. This can help us to avoid reacting impulsively or out of control, and instead respond to difficult situations with clarity and compassion.

It is also important for parents to communicate openly and honestly with their children about their emotions. By role-modeling healthy emotional expression, we can teach our children how to manage their own feelings in a positive way. Encouraging children to talk about their emotions, offering support and validation, and helping them to develop coping skills can help them to navigate the ups and downs of life with resilience and confidence. By recognizing the signs of stress, developing healthy coping mechanisms, and regulating our emotions in a constructive manner, we can create a positive and nurturing environment for our families. By practicing mindfulness, communicating openly with our children, and seeking support when needed, we can become more resilient and better equipped to handle the challenges of parenthood. Remember, it is okay to ask for help and take care of yourself - you deserve it.

- Building strong parent-child relationships through mindfulness

Building strong parent-child relationships through mindfulness is a topic that has gained significant attention in recent years as more research continues to emerge on the benefits of mindfulness practices for both children and parents. Mindfulness is defined as the ability to be fully present in the moment, to be aware of one's thoughts and feelings without judgment, and to cultivate a sense of compassion and acceptance towards oneself and others. When applied to parent-child relationships, mindfulness can help parents and children develop a deeper understanding of each other, communicate more effectively, and build stronger bonds based on trust and mutual respect.

One of the key principles of mindfulness is the idea of being fully present in the moment. For many parents, the demands of everyday life can make it difficult to truly be present with their children. Between work, household chores, and other responsibilities, it can be easy to get caught up in the busyness of daily life and forget to take the time to connect with our children on a deeper level. By practicing mindfulness, parents can learn to slow down, tune into their children's needs and emotions, and be more attentive and responsive to their cues. This can help parents to better understand their children's perspectives and support them in navigating the challenges they face.

Mindfulness can also help parents and children communicate more effectively. By practicing mindfulness, parents can learn to listen more actively and empathetically to their children's thoughts and feelings, without jumping to conclusions or rushing to judgment. This can help parents to foster open and honest communication with their children, which is essential for building trust and strengthening the parent-child bond. When children feel heard and understood by their parents, they are more likely to share their thoughts and feelings openly, leading to greater emotional intimacy and connection within the family.

Another important aspect of building strong parent-child relationships through mindfulness is fostering a sense of compassion and acceptance towards oneself and others. Parenting can be challenging and stressful at times, and it is easy for parents to become overwhelmed or frustrated with themselves or their children. By practicing self-compassion and acceptance, parents can learn to be kinder and gentler towards themselves, which can in turn lead to greater patience and understanding in their interactions with their children. Similarly, teaching children to practice self-compassion and acceptance can help them to develop a sense of resilience and self-worth, which are essential for healthy development and well-being.

In addition to the benefits of mindfulness for individual parents and children, research has shown that mindfulness practices can also have a positive impact on the parent-child relationship as a whole. Studies have found that parents who practice mindfulness report feeling more attuned to their children's needs, more satisfied with their parenting skills, and more confident in their ability to navigate the challenges of parenthood. Similarly, children of mindful parents tend to have better emotional regulation, higher self-esteem, and stronger social connections, which can contribute to more positive parent-child interactions and stronger bonds within the family. By practicing mindfulness, parents can learn to be more present, attentive, and empathetic in their interactions with their children, leading to greater emotional intimacy and trust within the family. Mindfulness can also help parents and children communicate more effectively, cultivate compassion and acceptance towards themselves and each other, and ultimately build stronger bonds based on mutual respect and love. By incorporating mindfulness practices into their daily lives, parents can create a more nurturing and supportive environment for their children to thrive and grow.

Chapter 19: Cultivating Joy and Happiness

- FINDING JOY IN THE present moment

In today's fast-paced world, many people find themselves constantly thinking about the future or dwelling on the past. This can lead to feelings of stress, anxiety, and dissatisfaction with life. However, research has shown that finding joy in the present moment can lead to greater overall happiness and well-being. By focusing on the here and now, we can cultivate a sense of gratitude, contentment, and peace that can have a profound impact on our mental and emotional health.

One of the most effective ways to find joy in the present moment is to practice mindfulness. Mindfulness is the practice of being fully present and aware of our thoughts, feelings, and sensations in each moment. By paying attention to the present moment without judgment, we can cultivate a greater sense of clarity, focus, and calm. This can help us to let go of worries about the future or regrets about the past, and instead, focus on what is happening right now.

Another way to find joy in the present moment is to engage in activities that bring us joy and fulfillment. This could be anything from spending time with loved ones, pursuing a hobby or passion, or simply taking a walk in nature. By focusing on what brings us joy in the present moment, we can cultivate a sense of purpose and meaning in our lives. This can help us to feel more connected to ourselves and others, and to experience greater levels of happiness and satisfaction.

Finding joy in the present moment also involves practicing gratitude and appreciation for the little things in life. By taking the time to notice and savor the small moments of beauty, kindness, and joy that surround us each day, we can cultivate a greater sense of gratitude and appreciation for our lives. This can help us to shift our focus away from what is lacking or missing in our lives, and instead, focus on the abundance and blessings that are already present.

In addition to practicing mindfulness, engaging in activities that bring us joy, and practicing gratitude, it is also important to cultivate a positive and optimistic mindset. By focusing on the good in our lives and looking for opportunities for growth and learning in each moment, we can cultivate a greater sense of optimism and resilience. This can help us to navigate life's challenges with grace and confidence, and to approach each day with a sense of hope and possibility. By practicing mindfulness, engaging in activities that bring us joy, practicing gratitude, and cultivating a positive mindset, we can learn to appreciate and savor the beauty and blessings that are already present in our lives. By focusing on the here and now, we can experience a greater sense of peace, contentment, and fulfillment that can have a lasting impact on our mental and emotional health. So, let us embrace the present moment with open hearts and minds, and find joy in the simple pleasures of life.

- Increasing happiness through mindfulness practices

In recent years, there has been a growing interest in the field of mindfulness and its potential to increase happiness and well-being. Mindfulness, which has its roots in ancient meditation practices, involves paying attention to the present moment in a non-judgmental way. By cultivating awareness of our thoughts, feelings, and bodily sensations, we can develop a greater sense of clarity, peace, and contentment in our lives.

One of the key ways in which mindfulness can increase happiness is by helping individuals to break free from the grip of negative thought patterns. Many of us are prone to getting caught up in rumination, worry, and self-criticism, which can erode our sense of well-being. By practicing mindfulness, we can learn to observe these thoughts without getting entangled in them, allowing us to let go of unhelpful narratives and create space for more positive and constructive ways of thinking.

Moreover, mindfulness can also help us to cultivate a greater sense of gratitude and appreciation for the present moment. In our fast-paced and often chaotic world, it can be easy to get caught up in a cycle of striving for more and better, without taking the time to savor the simple joys and blessings that are already present in our lives. By bringing mindful awareness to our everyday experiences, we can learn to fully engage with the beauty and richness of each moment, leading to a greater sense of fulfillment and happiness.

Furthermore, mindfulness can also help us to develop greater emotional resilience and regulation. In the face of life's inevitable challenges and setbacks, it is natural to experience a range of emotions, from sadness and anger to fear and anxiety. However, by practicing mindfulness, we can learn to approach these emotions with a sense of openness and acceptance, rather than trying to avoid or suppress them. This can help us to become more in tune with our inner emotional landscape, leading to greater self-awareness and the ability to respond to difficult situations with greater wisdom and compassion.

Additionally, mindfulness can also foster greater connection and compassion towards others. By cultivating a sense of presence and kindness in our interactions with others, we can deepen our relationships and create a more positive and supportive social environment. Through practices such as loving-kindness meditation, we can develop a sense of empathy and goodwill towards all beings, fostering a sense of interconnectedness and unity that can enhance our sense of well-being and happiness. By bringing awareness and presence to our thoughts, emotions, and experiences, we can cultivate a greater sense of clarity, gratitude, resilience, and connection that can enrich our lives and bring us greater joy and contentment. Through regular practice and dedication, we can harness the transformative potential of mindfulness to live more fully and authentically, and to find greater peace and fulfillment in the present moment.

- Nurturing a positive and content mindset

Having a positive and content mindset is essential for overall well-being and success in life. It is the foundation upon which we build our thoughts, emotions, and actions. A positive mindset can help us navigate through life's challenges with resilience and optimism, while a content mindset allows us to appreciate and savor the present moment. In this article, we will explore the importance of nurturing a positive and content mindset, as well as provide practical tips and strategies to help cultivate this mindset in our daily lives.

One of the key benefits of having a positive and content mindset is improved mental and emotional well-being. When we approach life with a positive attitude, we are better able to cope with stress, anxiety, and other negative emotions. Research has shown that individuals with a positive mindset are more resilient in the face of adversity and have lower rates of depression and anxiety. Similarly, a content mindset allows us to experience greater levels of satisfaction and fulfillment in our daily lives. By focusing on the present moment and cultivating a sense of gratitude for what we have, we can enhance our overall sense of well-being and happiness.

In addition to improving mental and emotional well-being, a positive and content mindset can also have a positive impact on our physical health. Studies have shown that individuals with a positive outlook on life are more likely to engage in healthy behaviors such as exercise, proper nutrition, and getting an adequate amount of sleep. These behaviors can help reduce the risk of developing chronic diseases such as heart disease, diabetes, and obesity. Furthermore, a positive mindset has been linked to a stronger immune system and faster recovery from illness and injury. By nurturing a positive and content mindset, we can improve our overall health and well-being.

Nurturing a positive and content mindset involves making a conscious effort to shift our thinking patterns and beliefs towards a more optimistic and appreciative perspective. One of the first steps in cultivating this mindset is to practice mindfulness and self-awareness. Mindfulness involves being fully present in the moment and non-judgmentally observing our thoughts, emotions, and sensations. By practicing mindfulness, we can become more aware of our thought patterns and make conscious choices to redirect negative or unhelpful thoughts towards more positive and empowering ones. This can help break the cycle of negative thinking and cultivate a more positive mindset.

Another important aspect of nurturing a positive and content mindset is practicing gratitude. Gratitude involves acknowledging and appreciating the good things in our lives, no matter how big or small. Research has shown that individuals who practice gratitude on a regular basis experience higher levels of well-being, happiness, and satisfaction with life. By cultivating a sense of gratitude, we can shift our focus from what we lack to what we have, leading to a more positive and content mindset. One way to practice gratitude is to keep a gratitude journal and write down three things we are grateful for each day.

This simple practice can help reframe our perspective and cultivate a sense of appreciation for the abundance in our lives.

In addition to mindfulness and gratitude, engaging in positive and uplifting activities can also help nurture a positive and content mindset. Surrounding ourselves with positive influences such as supportive friends and family members, inspirational books and quotes, and uplifting music and art can help reinforce a positive outlook on life. Engaging in activities that bring us joy and fulfillment, such as hobbies, exercise, and spending time in nature, can also help boost our mood and cultivate a more positive mindset. By incorporating these activities into our daily routine, we can create a more positive and content state of mind.

It is important to remember that nurturing a positive and content mindset is a continuous process that requires effort and intention. It is normal to experience ups and downs in our mood and outlook on life, but by practicing mindfulness, gratitude, and engaging in positive activities, we can gradually shift towards a more positive and content mindset. By cultivating a positive and content mindset, we can improve our mental, emotional, and physical well-being, and experience greater levels of fulfillment and happiness in our daily lives.

Chapter 20: Conclusion

- SUMMARY OF KEY MINDFULNESS practices

Mindfulness is a practice that involves bringing one's attention to the present moment in a non-judgmental and accepting way. It has gained popularity in recent years for its numerous mental and physical health benefits. There are several key mindfulness practices that can help individuals cultivate a greater sense of awareness and presence in their daily lives.

One of the fundamental mindfulness practices is mindful breathing. This involves focusing on the sensation of the breath as it enters and leaves the body. By paying attention to the breath, individuals can anchor themselves in the present moment and calm the mind. Mindful breathing can be practiced anywhere and at any time, making it a versatile technique for reducing stress and promoting relaxation.

Another important mindfulness practice is body scan meditation. This involves systematically moving attention through different parts of the body, noticing any sensations or tensions that arise without judgment. Body scan meditation can help individuals become more attuned to the physical signals of stress or discomfort in their bodies, allowing them to release tension and promote relaxation.

Mindful walking is another key mindfulness practice that involves paying attention to the sensations of walking, such as the feeling of the feet contacting the ground and the movement of the body. Walking mindfully can help individuals slow down and become more present in their surroundings, allowing them to appreciate the simple act of walking and connect with the world around them.

Mindful eating is a practice that involves bringing full attention to the experience of eating, noticing the tastes, textures, and smells of the food without distractions. By eating mindfully, individuals can savor their meals more fully and cultivate a greater awareness of their eating habits. This can help prevent overeating and promote healthier eating behaviors.

Mindful listening is a practice that involves giving full attention to the person speaking, without judgment or the urge to interrupt. By listening mindfully, individuals can deepen their understanding of others and cultivate stronger relationships. Mindful listening can also help individuals become more present in their interactions and improve their communication skills.

In addition to these key mindfulness practices, there are many other ways to cultivate mindfulness in daily life. Mindful journaling, for example, involves writing about one's thoughts and feelings in a non-judgmental way, allowing individuals to gain insight into their mental patterns and emotions. Mindful movement practices, such as yoga or tai chi, can also help individuals become more present in their bodies and cultivate a greater sense of awareness. By incorporating key mindfulness practices into their daily routines, individuals can cultivate a greater sense of awareness, presence, and compassion in their lives.

- Reflection on personal growth and well-being

Reflection on personal growth and well-being is a crucial aspect of self-improvement and self-awareness. It involves taking the time to assess one's strengths, weaknesses, values, and goals in order to identify areas for growth and development. By reflecting on our experiences, thoughts, and behaviors, we can gain valuable insights into our own beliefs and motivations, as well as the impact they have on our overall well-being. This process of self-reflection allows us to make more informed decisions, set meaningful goals, and ultimately live a more fulfilling and purposeful life.

Personal growth and well-being are interconnected concepts that encompass a wide range of dimensions, including physical, emotional, mental, and spiritual aspects of our being. Achieving growth and well-being involves taking care of ourselves holistically, addressing all these dimensions in a balanced and integrated manner. This means paying attention to our physical health by exercising regularly, eating nutritious foods, getting enough sleep, and practicing self-care. It also involves nurturing our emotional and mental well-being by cultivating positive relationships, managing stress effectively, and practicing mindfulness and self-reflection.

In order to foster personal growth and well-being, it is important to cultivate self-awareness and mindfulness. Self-awareness involves being conscious of our thoughts, emotions, and behaviors, as well as their impact on ourselves and others. By developing self-awareness, we can gain insights into our patterns of thinking and reacting, identify areas for improvement, and make more intentional choices in our daily lives. Mindfulness, on the other hand, involves being fully present in the moment, paying attention to our thoughts and feelings without judgment, and cultivating a sense of calm and inner peace. By practicing mindfulness, we can reduce stress, enhance our focus and concentration, and improve our overall well-being.

Another key aspect of personal growth and well-being is the importance of setting and achieving meaningful goals. Setting goals gives us a sense of direction and purpose, motivating us to take action and make positive changes in our lives. Whether it's a career goal, a fitness goal, a personal development goal, or a relationship goal, having clear objectives helps us stay focused and committed to our growth and well-being. Achieving goals also provides a sense of accomplishment and satisfaction, boosting our self-confidence and self-esteem.

In addition to setting goals, it is important to cultivate a growth mindset in order to maximize personal growth and well-being. A growth mindset is the belief that our abilities and intelligence can be developed through effort, perseverance, and learning from failures. This mindset encourages us to embrace challenges, seek out new experiences, and view setbacks as opportunities for growth and learning. By adopting a growth mindset, we can overcome obstacles, develop new skills, and achieve our full potential in all areas of our lives.

Self-care is another essential component of personal growth and well-being. Self-care involves taking deliberate actions to meet our own physical, emotional, and mental needs, and recharge our energy reserves. It can include activities such as exercise, meditation, journaling, spending time in nature, getting a massage, or simply taking a break to relax and unwind. Self-care is not selfish or indulgent; it is an essential practice that allows us to replenish our energy, reduce stress, and enhance our overall well-being. By prioritizing self-care, we can build resilience, prevent burnout, and maintain a healthy work-life balance.

In closing, personal growth and well-being are ongoing processes that require reflection, practice, and continuous effort. It is important to regularly assess our progress, adjust our goals and priorities, and seek support from others when needed. By staying committed to our growth and well-being, we can create a life that is meaningful, fulfilling, and aligned with our values and aspirations. As we continue to invest in our own personal development, we not only enhance our own well-being but also contribute positively to the well-being of those around us. Through reflection, self-awareness, goal-setting, a growth mindset, self-care, and ongoing commitment, we can cultivate personal growth and well-being in our lives and create a positive impact on the world.

- Commitment to continued mindfulness practice for mental well-being.

Mindfulness practice has long been recognized for its numerous benefits for mental well-being. Defined as the act of paying attention to the present moment in a non-judgmental way, mindfulness has been shown to reduce stress, increase emotional regulation, and improve overall psychological well-being. In today's fast-paced and often overwhelming world, maintaining a commitment to continued mindfulness practice is more important than ever.

One of the key reasons why ongoing mindfulness practice is crucial for mental well-being is its ability to reduce stress and anxiety. Mindfulness allows individuals to focus on the present moment rather than worrying about the past or future. By cultivating a sense of presence and awareness, individuals can better manage their thoughts and emotions, leading to a decrease in overall stress levels. Research has consistently shown that regular mindfulness practice can lower cortisol levels, the hormone associated with stress, and decrease symptoms of anxiety.

Furthermore, continued mindfulness practice can improve emotional regulation and increase overall resilience. By learning to observe one's thoughts and emotions without self-judgment, individuals can develop a sense of inner peace and stability. This enhanced emotional regulation can help individuals navigate difficult situations with greater ease and respond to challenges in a more balanced and adaptive manner. Studies have also found that regular mindfulness practice can increase grey matter in areas of the brain associated with emotional regulation, leading to improved mood and overall psychological well-being.

In addition to reducing stress and improving emotional regulation, continued mindfulness practice can also enhance cognitive function and overall mental clarity. Mindfulness has been shown to improve attention and focus, allowing individuals to better concentrate on tasks and activities. By training the mind to be more present and attentive, individuals can experience a greater sense of mental clarity and purpose. Research has also found that regular mindfulness practice can increase cognitive flexibility and creativity, as individuals learn to approach situations with an open and non-judgmental mindset.

Despite the numerous benefits of mindfulness practice for mental well-being, maintaining a commitment to ongoing practice can be challenging. In today's busy world, it can be easy to get caught up in the demands of daily life and neglect our mental health. However, by prioritizing mindfulness practice and integrating it into our daily routines, we can reap the long-term benefits for our mental well-being. Setting aside just a few minutes each day to engage in mindful activities such as meditation, deep breathing, or body scan can make a significant difference in our overall mental health.

To support continued mindfulness practice, it can be helpful to establish a structured routine and set realistic goals for practice. Whether it's dedicating a specific time each day to engage in mindfulness activities or committing to attending a weekly mindfulness class, having a routine can help to maintain consistency and motivation. Setting achievable goals, such as practicing mindfulness for a certain amount of time each day or week, can also provide a sense of accomplishment and progress. By approaching mindfulness practice with a sense of commitment and dedication, individuals can build a strong foundation for improved mental well-being. By reducing stress, improving emotional regulation, and enhancing cognitive function, mindfulness practice can have profound effects on our overall psychological health. Despite the challenges of maintaining ongoing practice, prioritizing mindfulness and integrating it into our daily routines can lead to long-lasting benefits for our mental well-being. By approaching mindfulness practice with dedication and consistency, individuals can cultivate a sense of inner peace, resilience, and clarity that can greatly enhance their quality of life.